BLOODY BRITISH HISTORY

HISTORY

HEREFORD

DAVID PHELPS

The
History
Press

The History Press
The Mill, Brimscombe Port
Stroud, Gloucestershire, GL5 2QG
www.thehistorypress.co.uk

Reprinted 2013

British Library Cataloguing in Publication Data.
A catalogue record for this book is available from the British Library.

ISBN 978 0 7524 8090 9

Typesetting and origination by The History Press
Printed and bound by TJ International Ltd, Padstow, Cornwall

CONTENTS

ACKNOWLEDGEMENTS

MY SPECIAL THANKS to David Whitehead for acting as my historical adviser; any inaccuracies are down to my own pig-headedness. Thanks also to Rob Soldat for his knowledge of the border, Jacqueline Jonson and Gwilym Rees of the Woolhope Club and the staff of the local section of Hereford Library, Hereford Cathedral Library and Rhys Griffith, Richard Wade and Marcus Buffrey of Hereford Record Office. My gratitude also to the members of Much Dewchurch and Newent story circles for listening to these stories as they were developing and to Cate Ludlow and her colleagues at The History Press for suggesting the project.

Unless otherwise credited, illustrations are sourced via the publisher.

INTRODUCTION

'He who cannot draw on three thousand years
of history is living from hand to mouth.'

Goethe

THE COUNTY OF Hereford is undergoing a transformation. From earning its living mostly through agriculture, as it has done for many centuries, it will become a centre of investment to rival the South East – or at least, that is the vision of those currently in charge of its destiny. No one would argue with prosperity but, as the following pages show, one man's prosperity can be ten people's desperation: all the more important, then, to know the county's heritage, so that it can be protected during the transformation.

Herefordshire has a complex history and it would be impossible to reflect all the complexity in this short book but I hope it will whet your appetite and provide a sketch map to encourage further exploration.

2,000 BC

THE ROTHERWAS RIBBON

DURING THE BUILDING of the Rotherwas Access Road a curving line of stones was found between the River Wye and Dinedor Hill. Later carbon-dating methods suggest that this was placed here in the Neolithic period.

The stones had been brought from a ridge about half a kilometre away, fire cracked (heated and then dropped into cold water to shatter, the earliest known example of this practice) and laid in a sinuous series of curves. The stones were interspersed with quartz pebbles so that, in sunlight, the ribbon would have glinted like a large white snake on the hillside and, in the moonlight, it would have glowed as if the nearby river was climbing up the hill.

The stones were only one layer thick, so this was not a trackway. However, what it was the archaeologists were unwilling to surmise, putting it down to ritual or ceremony (i.e. we have no idea). They did say that the find was unique and as significant as Stonehenge. Perhaps Herefordshire was as ritually important as the Wiltshire Plain?

However, the council was determined that the new road must go ahead. Eight members of the public, including an octogenarian war hero, were arrested in the council chamber for criminal trespass because they wanted the matter discussed openly. The case was only dropped when a leading firm of civil rights solicitors became involved.

The Ribbon was eventually covered over and the £12 million new road built over it. This stretch of tarmac is now recognised as one of the quietest stretches of road in the county.

The Rotherwas Access Road, now covering the Rotherwas Ribbon. (David Phelps)

AD 43

CARADOC

CARADOC – OR Caratacus, as the Romans, who could not stand people to have non-Latin names, called him – was a leader of the Catuvellauni tribe, who lived in what is now Hertfordshire, Bedfordshire and north Cambridgeshire. British tribal boundaries were always quite fluid and Caradoc was intent on expanding his, at the expense of his neighbours.

He had considerable success against the Atrebates of Hampshire and Surrey. So much so that their leaders saw no option but to ask the Romans for help, in the same way that the Kuwaitis called for help from the Americans when they were invaded by Iraq in 1990 – and we all know where that led.

Emperor Claudius must have smiled when he received the request. Though a magnificent PR campaign by Julius Caesar had persuaded the Roman people that his attempted invasion a century before had been a success, Claudius knew better. With the Germans being a continual trial on his eastern border, this was a chance to expand the northern one.

Caradoc might have been a skilled commander against other tribes, but he was no match for the Legions of Rome. He was soundly defeated at the Battle of Medway and fled, while a new tribal leadership sued for peace. There were many Britons who thought the Romans were a good thing anyway. There had been trade with them for many centuries and the elites especially valued the luxury goods this provided. What did it matter if they had to make their farmers pay more taxes?

Caradoc headed west, to Herefordshire, where there were more hillforts than any other district. We now know that the term 'hillfort' is a bit of a misnomer: they seem to have served many different purposes, from the place where people would go to perform seasonal ceremonies to the home

Nineteenth-century interpretation of Caradoc meeting Claudius.

British Camp, one of the last stands of Caradoc. (David Phelps)

of the chieftain. Many of them would have been completely impractical as defensive positions. But Caradoc was heading for British Camp, on the Malverns, which was a highly defensible fort. The local Dobunni tribe were generally in favour of the Romans, but there were enough young hot heads who wanted to make a name for themselves by resisting the invaders. Caradoc strengthened the walls, planning to use the camp as an impregnable base from which he could carry out guerrilla warfare.

Certainly it must have looked impregnable to the Roman commander, Publius Ostorius Scapula, when he saw it, but his men, from the battle-hardened IX and XX Legions, convinced him that they could take it. In *testudo* or tortoise formation – shields above their heads, to neutralise the arrows and stones rained down on them from above – the soldiers penetrated the defences and the battle became hand-to-hand. The Britons, with their free-form fighting style, were no match for the tight discipline of the Legions and there was a bloody slaughter, the Romans never too keen on taking prisoners.

Caradoc, like all good leaders, had a Plan B. Once more he fled the battle and headed for Croft Ambrey in north-west Herefordshire, close to the territory of the Silures, who had no love for the Romans. But history repeated itself and Caradoc was forced to run again, this time to Caer Caradoc in Shropshire, where he was joined not only by the local Cornovii but also Ordovices from North Wales, who were always ready for a fight.

But the Romans were not going to alter a winning formula. Another slaughter followed. Leaving his wife and children to potential slavery, Caradoc fled north, to the land of the Brigantes. But their queen, Cartimandua (ancient Briton was an

Testudo formation. (With kind permission of the Thomas Fisher Rare Book Library, University of Toronto)

equal-opportunities society) was not going to risk the anger of the Romans for this serial loser. She had him chained and sent to the Romans.

Caradoc and his family were sent to Rome, where he should have been strangled as part of Claudius's triumph for conquering southern Britain. However, according to the historian Tacitus he made an impassioned speech in his own defence:

> I had horses, men, arms, and wealth: what wonder if I was unwilling to lose them? If you wish to command everyone, does it really follow that everyone should accept your slavery? If I were now being handed over as one who had surrendered immediately, neither my fortune nor your glory would have achieved brilliance. It is also true that in my case any reprisal will be followed by oblivion. On the other hand, if you preserve me safe and sound, I shall be an eternal example of your clemency.

Claudius was so impressed that he pardoned Caradoc and allowed him to live a life of luxury in Rome for the rest of his days.

One tradition says that Caradoc converted to Christianity and returned to Britain to convert his people from their pagan ways, though this is probably a later, monkish, invention. Today Caradoc, the mighty war leader, is probably best remembered in the song *The Court of King Caratacus*, made popular by Rolf Harris in the 1960s.

THE ROMANS IN HEREFORDSHIRE

It has been generally thought that, at the time of the Roman invasion, Herefordshire was primeval forest. However, recent tree-pollen analysis suggests that this had been largely cleared by as early as 4,500 BC and that, at this time, there was already a much greater level of human settlement than had previously been surmised. The pre-Roman British culture was of a higher order of civilization than has often been credited.

Even after the defeat of Caradoc, this was still the Wild West to the Romans, as the Silures were still resisting their rule. As today having oil can be a curse rather than a blessing, the lead, gold, silver and copper known to be in Wales meant that the Romans were determined to suppress resistance at whatever cost. A war grave found at Sutton Walls near Marden, where skeletons show the marks of sharp-edged weapons, show how brutal this suppression could be.

After some thirty years of guerrilla warfare the Romans had achieved some form of peace, but were still wary of trouble. An important road, Watling Street, linked the large military bases of Caerleon and Chester, passing through

Reconstruction of British round hut, Clearwell, Gloucestershire. (David Phelps)

Herefordshire. Along this road towns sprang up. Leintwardine (Bravonium) in the north seems to have principally been a military supply depot, whereas Kenchester (Magnis), the largest Roman settlement in the county, had a more civilian bias. Built near the large hillfort at Credenhill, perhaps it also served to encourage some of the local elite to come down from their draughty hillside to the warm baths of Roman life. (Though modern reconstructions have shown that Celtic round houses could be very cosy places.)

Weston-under-Penyard (Ariconium) was an industrial centre, especially for iron smelting, linked to the nearby Forest of Dean. As was usual with the Romans, they rewarded the chiefs who had accepted Roman rule and used them to administer the area. There are luxury villas at Wellington, Putley, Bishopstone, Walterstone and Whitchurch where these chiefs lived in a style to which they rapidly became accustomed.

For over 300 years a relative peace settled over the area. But, as empires must, the Roman empire fell into decadence and decay. Instead of looking for new conquests, the elite started fighting within themselves and control of the provinces was weakened. When governors of Britain started getting involved, taking the Legions away to Rome to try and make themselves Emperors, the Romano-British realised that it was time to take the law back into their own hands.

AD 460

ARTHUR

KING ARTHUR'S MOTHER was born in Herefordshire. Admittedly many historians doubt the existence of a real King Arthur but, if he did exist, Herefordshire, as the home of one branch of Welsh royal blood, has more claims than most as a potential site of his birth.

The first literary reference to Arthur is in the late sixth-century poem *Y Gododdin*, which refers to a valiant warrior 'though he is no Arthur'. Other Welsh sources point to one particular war leader called Arthur who held back Saxon influence through his military victories.

At the end of Roman rule Britain split up into various warring kingdoms. Herefordshire was divided in two, with the 'Welsh' Kingdom of Ergyng to the west and the Magonsaete tribal area to the east, with the boundary roughly following the line of the River Wye. According to the legend, Peibio, King of Ergyng, attempted to execute his daughter because she was going to have an illegitimate child, but mother and baby miraculously survived both drowning and burning. Clearly the child was destined for great things. This child, Dyfrig (water baby) later renounced his kingship and devoted himself to the Church, where he was known as St Dubricius. Tradition has it that he was

the uncle of Arthur and immensely wise. He was supposed to have crowned his nephew and has been linked to Merlin, the legendary counsellor who was responsible for Arthur's rise to kingship.

Peibio also had a son called Cyfan, whose own son was called Gwrgant Mawr. One of Gwrgant's daughters was called Ygerne (after whom the Eign Brook in Hereford is named, although this has now gone as part of Herefordshire Council's flood alleviation scheme to protect their new shopping mall). She married Meuric ap Tewdric, whom the Tudors claimed as an ancestor. Meuric was given the honorific title Uther Pendragon, meaning fierce war leader. He, of course, was the father of Arthur.

Arthur grew into a mighty warrior who protected his people against the encroachments of the Saxons. Croft Ambrey in the north of the county has been claimed as one of his fortresses, although no post-Roman archaeology has been found there. The Doward, in the south of the county, is claimed to be the site of one of his great battles, where he defeated and killed King Vortigern. Certainly there is a place at the bottom of the hill still called the Slaughter.

There are other places that have been closely linked to Arthur's story. It was a long-held belief in this area that Caradoc

Above *Visions of Arthur: the knights of the Round Table about to start the hunt for the Holy Grail. (LC-USZ62-133641)*

Right *A nineteenth-century portrayal of the fight between Arthur and Mordred.*

Court, near Ross, was the home of Caradoc-of-the-Strong Arm, one of Arthur's knights. Old Welsh records suggest that Caradoc was the son of Gwrgant, Arthur's uncle.

Wormelow Tump, south of the city of Hereford, was the site, according to the seventh-century chronicler Nennius, of one of the 'Marvels of Britain'. It was the mound to mark the burial site of Anir, Arthur's son, killed by his own father for treason. If measured, the mound would never be the same length twice. It was lost as part of Herefordshire Council's road-widening scheme in 1896.

West of Hereford is the village of Mordiford. Bruce Copplestone-Crow, in *Herefordshire Place Names*, describes its name as 'unexplained'. Locals have no such problem, believing it means Mordred's Ford, and that the green dragon that was emblazoned on the side of the church until 1811 was his banner. More mundane historians suggest that it was a wyvern, part of the coat of arms of St Guthlac's Priory, the owners of the parish in the Middle Ages. However, Guthlac, a relatively obscure saint, was described as of Welsh royal blood. The original priory was based on the site of the present Castle Green in Hereford, and old Welsh manuscripts describe it as one of the earliest of Christian sites, set up in the fifth century, long before Guthlac's time, when the land belonged to Geraint, Arthur's cousin.

Naturally, as we are dealing with the Dark Ages, much of the above is supposition, based on later chronicles. However, it is intriguing to think that the legendary figure of King Arthur had close links to Herefordshire.

ANGLO-SAXON INVASION?

Since the Venomous Bede wrote his *Ecclesiastical History of the English People* back in the eighth century it has been accepted that, after the Romans left, hordes of Germanic tribes invaded from Denmark, Saxony and Jutland, massacred the native population or drove them to the west. As archaeological investigations have failed to find mass burials that would prove this point, this view has been tempered into one where the invading Anglo-Saxons conquered but lived alongside the Celts in an apartheid system.

However, latterly, historians have argued that such a view is much too simplistic. Francis Pryor, well known from his appearances on *Time Team*, has been particularly outspoken, believing that the 'invasion' was in fact a slow and largely peaceful process, an infusion of culture rather than wholesale genocide.

Yet we speak English and not Welsh, the latter language assumed to be close to that spoken by the native population at that time. This seems to have happened only in the ninth century when Wessex bureaucrats wanted standardisation, as bureaucrats always do. Therefore perhaps the Anglo-Saxon invasion was very similar to the Norman Conquest, with a small elite replacing the local aristocracy, while leaving the peasants, who would have to do all the work, largely untouched.

New DNA techniques do seem to show that there were substantially fewer Anglo-Saxon migrants than was originally expected. Stephen Oppenheimer, in his book *Origins of the British*, argues that, from DNA analysis, at least two thirds of English people have direct ancestors that have been on these islands since just after the last Ice Age. He argues that, as the ice retreated and the climate improved, the Celts left their refuge near the Pyrenees, some of them travelling along the shoreline until they reached western Britain. Another Germanic group, from their refuge near the Caucasus, travelled via Russia and Scandinavia across the then dry North Sea, until they arrived in eastern Britain. If so, the two groups might have met somewhere along the River Wye, so that the old fault line in the county, between English and Welsh, goes back not 1,500 years but 10,000.

AD 780

OFFA'S DYKE

THOUGH WE CALL it the Dark Ages because there are so few written records from this time, rather than because it was a period of complete anarchy, life in this era would undoubtedly have been pretty tough for the ordinary people. With no centralised authority, each ambitious warlord would attempt to seize the largest territory possible and it would have been all too easy for farmers to become collateral damage. Tactics and morals were as underhand as any seen in corporate boardrooms today, but there would be no index-linked pension for the loser: only death in a bloody battlefield.

Territories were ever-changing but we might get some idea of the Magonsaete boundaries from the diocese of Hereford, as ancient sees tended to follow tribal boundaries. If so, it extended up as far as Shrewsbury and down to the Forest of Dean. The Kingdom of the Magonsaete was one of the smaller kingdoms and depended on its continued existence on weakness and political instability within its bigger neighbours. All this changed in 757 when King Aethelbald of Mercia was assassinated by his own bodyguard. The King's cousin, Offa, was not going to miss this opportunity. He set about disposing of any other cousin who might challenge his authority until he was the last male member of the royal family still to have a head on his shoulders.

Offa was a determined warrior and a skilled politician. Little kingdoms such as the Magonsaete and the Hwicce of Worcestershire and Gloucestershire were soon swallowed up. What he could not achieve by warfare he achieved by skilful negotiation, often marrying his daughters to other kings to create political allegiances. At the height of his power his domain stretched from the Mersey in the north to the south coast, and from the Welsh border to the Fens. Many historians have argued that he was the first man who could call himself King of the English, with some justification. Yet he seemed to be guided not by any vision of a united island but by the fact that he just could not stop himself from embarking on more conquests.

But he did face one insurmountable problem on his western boundary: the Princes of Powys. He did not have the resources to overcome them and there were constant cattle raids and incursions. So he hit on a grandiose solution: the Dyke. It was not an original idea – there was already a small ditch and rampart to mark the boundary – but he intended to make a statement. The Dyke, when built, was 27 metres wide and 8 metres high. It is a tribute to Offa's power that he could order such a thing created, though probably the men he persuaded to dig it did not feel that way.

It used to be thought that it extended from Chepstow to Prestatyn, but the latest archaeology suggests that it only went from Rushcock Hill in Herefordshire to Mold in Flintshire, which might have been where the worst incursions occurred. Nor was it permanently defended, as was Hadrian's Wall. It would, however, have acted as a serious impediment to cattle raiding, as anyone who has tried getting cows and horses down a 30ft drop will testify.

CHRISTIANITY IN HEREFORDSHIRE

The story goes that, in 595, Pope Gregory was being carried in his litter through a slave market in Rome when he saw some blond young men about to be sold. When he heard they were Angles he said, 'They are angels, not Angles,' and persuaded one of his senior civil servants, Augustine, to go to Britain to convert them from their heathen ways. This Augustine did very successfully by first showing the ruling elite the political advantages of conversion, so they in turn would tell the peasants to go and get baptised.

As far as many people in the Hereford area were concerned he need not have bothered because they were already Christian, especially in the west of the region. Celtic Christianity, coming from Ireland some time after the Romans left, had become a very different organisation from that now in Rome. It was less hierarchical, with no bishops, relying on monks living alone or in small groups to inspire the local population with their wisdom. It had a different way of calculating Easter and making a tonsure, the shaving of the head to mark a man as a priest. While the Roman Church shaved the top of the head, the Celtic Church shaved the front, which some people think harked back to a druidic practice to show a man had wisdom. Those of us of a certain age, whose hair is rapidly retreating, find this a comforting thought. St Dyfrig first tried the Roman Church but found it uncongenial and turned to the native version.

When the local Celtic monks heard that Augustine was approaching they went to see the wisest hermit they knew and asked his advice. 'When you meet him,' he replied, 'if he comes and meets you like a brother then you know he is a true man of God, but if he remains stubbornly seated then you should come away.' When the meeting took place, at Rock, on the Herefordshire/Worcester border, Augustine, as befitted his rank as Primate of southern Britain, remained in his chair. The Welsh refused to accept his rule or agree to the changes that he demanded. It was not until the Synod of Whitby in 664 that Roman practices were finally accepted in this part of the world.

AD 794

ST AETHELBERT

AETHELBERT BECAME KING of East Anglia while he was still a small child, after the death of his father Aethelred.

At the time East Anglia was a sub-kingdom, notionally independent but in reality tightly controlled by Offa of Mercia. But, as young men do, Aethelbert wanted to assert himself. He started issuing his own coins, something guaranteed to annoy Offa, who was determined to control the economy himself. Aethelbert did not take the hint. Three times Offa had to tell him to stop. Then, in 793, Vikings attacked the monastery of Lindisfarne in Northumbria, the first raid in an attack that would bring Anglo-Saxon civilization almost to its knees. Offa must have decided that he needed someone he could trust sitting on the throne of East Anglia.

It was well known that Offa would seal alliances by marrying his daughters to his fellow kings so, when Offa suggested that Aethelbert travel to Offa's palace at Sutton Walls to discuss the marriage between Aethelbert and Offa's daughter, it was an offer that the young man could not refuse. Fans of Mafia movies will know that being invited to the mansion of the big boss is not always a positive career move. So it proved for Aethelbert.

Leaving his sword and bodyguard at the door, Aethelbert eagerly rushed into the King's hall, expecting to meet his new bride. Instead, the door slammed behind him. As he turned, he would have just been aware of the glint of a sword before it bit into his neck and took his head clean off. The body collapsed, rolling along the floor and pumping blood into the rushes.

He was quickly buried in the swampy ground near Marden, but the deed played on Offa's mind, especially when Aethelbert appeared to one of Offa's thegns in a dream and demanded to be buried with greater respect. So the body was dug up and taken to the church at Fernlea, which is now Hereford. On the way the head fell off the cart, but it was retrieved by a blind man, whose sight – or so the legend claims – was instantly restored.

Some sources claim that Offa's wife persuaded him to murder Aethelbert because he refused her advances. Cynethryth does seem to have been a very powerful woman, her face appearing on some of Offa's coins, which is quite unprecedented, but this seems an unjustified calumny. Whatever the truth, however, the Church quickly declared Aethelbert a saint. His tomb thus became a site of pilgrimage, one so popular that it was the second most visited pilgrimage

St Aethelbert after his meeting with Offa.

destination after Canterbury. In AD 1000 the cathedral was dedicated to him and St Mary the Virgin.

With the Welsh problem at least partially solved by the construction of the Dyke and the throne of East Anglia now vacant, Offa moved to consolidate his power. He was in communication with the mighty Charlemagne, the Holy Roman Emperor, by whom he was treated as an equal. The beautiful coins of his reign point to the artful skill of this period and show strong Frankish influences. Offa's was not an ignorant, brutal court, but highly cultivated for its time. Such was his power that he could quarrel with the mighty Archbishop of Canterbury and expect the Pope, Adrian, to take his side. This led to the creation of a third Archbishopric, in Lichfield, near Offa's capital, Tamworth. When it came to succession planning, Offa therefore did not have to negotiate with Canterbury but simply order his Lichfield archbishop to crown his son, Ecgfrith. According to scholar Alcuin of York, he did, however, enforce this diplomacy with the point of a sword: 'For you know very well how much blood his father shed to secure the kingdom on his son.'

Offa was killed in 796, fighting the Welsh, possibly whilst trying to extend his Dyke further north. His son lasted just five months in the job before he was assassinated by a challenger to the throne. But this man did not have Offa's skills and, before long, once subservient kingdoms started reasserting their independence. Offa's Dyke ceased to be maintained. Eventually, Wessex proved stronger and better led and it was a man from the royal bloodline of that kingdom who would next proclaim himself King of all the English.

AD 911

AETHELFLAED

VIKING RAIDS INCREASED. Soon it was not just the east coast that was suffering. With their sturdy but shallow draught, longboats could travel along any navigable river. Until recently, one of Worcester Cathedral's most prized possessions was what they claimed was the skin of a Viking, killed in a raid on the city, flayed and the skin nailed to the cathedral door. Hereford, with its navigable Wye, was also subject to sudden raids, so it was not so easy for anyone to sleep easily in their beds.

By the middle of the ninth century the raids had changed their nature. No longer quick hit-and-run affairs for plunder, the Danish Viking armies started to come over and settle in Britain. Northumbria, East Anglia and eastern Mercia were conquered. In 878 even Alfred, the King of Wessex, was forced to flee and live as a hunted refugee in the marshy parts of Somerset. With him he took his eldest child, his eight-year-old daughter, Aethelflaed. No doubt it was in these terrible months that she learnt some of her father's military and diplomatic skills, which would stand her in good stead in the future.

From this lowest point Alfred was able to re-take his lost kingdom and halt the advance of the Danes. At the age of twenty Aethelflaed was married to the Earl of Mercia, Aethelred, creating a powerful block on any further Danish advances.

From the start Aethelflaed was no mere decorative diplomatic pawn but was involved in setting up treaties and being closely involved in the governance of Mercia. Aethelred may have been a sickly man and there has always been great speculation why the couple only had one child, a daughter, Aelfwynn. Some think this might have been because of Athelred's weakness, while others think it was because Aethelflaed had a difficult childbirth and would not let Aethelred come anywhere near her after that. Conspiracy theorists suggest that it was a plot to prevent there being any future heir for Mercia, paving the way for its eventual amalgamation with Wessex.

Alfred died in AD 899 and was succeeded by his son Edward the Elder. He, together with Aethelflaed and Athelred, continued his father's work in driving back the Danes. But, in 910, a large Danish army sailed into the Bristol Channel, landed and headed north. They 'harried' Herefordshire, destroying farms, taking crops and livestock and slaughtering or enslaving anyone they found. They are described as 'taking no small prey' – which meant that if you were a peasant your luck was out. Then the army moved north. Just outside

Saxon defences uncovered in Hereford. (David Phelps)

Wolverhampton they were met by an avenging army of men from Mercia and Wessex. The English outnumbered the Danes but their numbers were made up of the local militias, not as well trained or equipped as the Danes. However, because of their larger numbers they were able to out-flank the Danish shield wall and break it. The Danes were massacred. Three Danish chieftains were among the dead. Unfortunately Athelred was also mortally wounded and was carried back to Tamworth to die.

Aethelflaed now had two choices; she could retire to a nunnery, which was the normal ending for a nobleman's widow, or she could rule in her own right. Aethelflaed was Alfred's daughter, and she did not hesitate. In the next few years she consolidated the work of her father. Alfred's great invention was the burh, a fortified settlement to which people could run when the Danes attacked. This had worked in Wessex and now Aethelflaed set about fortifying Mercian towns, including Hereford, which became the most westerly burh. Hereford's boundaries, which roughly stretched from the New Bridge to West Street, along East Street and then down to the river, were marked by a ditch and a wooden palisade. Miraculously we can still see some traces of these timbers, behind shops at the corner of St Owen Street and Cantilupe Street, the only Saxon defences still known to be in existence.

In 914 another Danish army arrived in the Bristol Channel. They ravaged Gwent and captured the Bishop of Llandaff. They

A coin of Edward the Elder, who drove back the Danes alongside Aethelflaed.

then headed for Hereford, but were defeated by the militia from the town. Survivors fled to Flat Holm in the Bristol Channel, where they were starved to death by Aethelflaed's blockade. This was to be the last major Viking attack on England for sixty years.

Aethelflaed did not have only the Danes to deal with, but also the Welsh. In 916, in retribution for various incursions, she attacked the King of Brycheiniog, burned down his hall at Llangorse and took his wife and thirty-three other nobles hostage. Any more trouble and they would have their throats slit.

Aethelflaed, the Lady of the Mercians, died in 918 and was succeeded by her daughter Aelfwynn, then aged about twenty. Within the year she was persuaded to hand control of Mercia to her uncle, Edward, King of Wessex, and retire to a nunnery, where she could produce no heirs that would threaten Edward. So Mercia ceased to be even notionally independent and became part of what was increasingly being called England. Athelstan, Edward's son, who is often listed as the first King of England, was educated at Aethelflaed's court and must have been inspired by her example.

Perhaps Aethelflaed is best known these days from Bernard Cornwell's series of novels about Uhtred of Northumbria, where the hero is in love with this Saxon princess.

CREATION OF HEREFORDSHIRE

The area around Hereford seems to have originally been called Fernlea, a ferny clearing. However, by the time of Aethelflaed it was being called Hereford, the ford where an army could cross, an indication of its strategic importance.

There is some confusion as to when the first Bishop of Hereford was appointed, although it seems to have been at the end of the seventh century. It was a tribal diocese, covering the boundaries of the Magonsaete sub-kingdom, with a bishop moving around his flock rather than based at a cathedral.

When Aethelflaed created the burh of Hereford she needed a hinterland of agricultural land to maintain it. Hereford was assessed as needing 1,200 hides, roughly the size of the county in the Domesday survey. A hide is a variable unit of land sufficient to support a peasant and his household, which was the unit of choice for tax assessment in this period. It seems that the shire was originally created as a new division to support the local burh and that is why it does not have the same boundaries as the diocese. Other shires, such as Worcester, also based around an administrative burh, were created at the same time. Strangely there is no record of the area actually being referred to as Herefordshire until the beginning of the eleventh century, although this is most likely because of the loss of so much documentation from this period.

AD 1055

THE BATTLE OF HEREFORD

KING EDWARD THE Confessor had a problem, and the problem was the Welsh. The man he sent to sort out the problem was his nephew, Ralph, Earl of Hereford. Ralph was a hard man, a Norman, but Herefordshire was a very different place to the borderlands he was used to. The peasants were surly. That did not bother him, but even the local nobles laughed in his face when he told them he was going to build castles to protect the land in the Norman fashion and that he wanted them to fight on horseback, the way a proper knight fights. They had been trained on foot, in the shield wall, where brother fights beside brother.

All too soon the test came, in the shape of Gruffydd ap Llewellyn, now lord of North and South Wales, whose eyes turned to the rich farmland of Herefordshire.

October is the blood month, when the harvest is in and men, freed from their labour, think of the riches in other men's barns. In October they came, not just the Welsh but also men from Dublin, hordes of Vikings, intent on plunder, and also some Englishmen, men of Mercia, who hated the Normans and who now came to kill them and anyone who stood with them.

Ralph assembled his army, and rode out to face the approaching Welsh army, who were mustered barely a mile outside the city at a place we now call White Cross. However, as the Hereford army reached the Welsh lines, screams began to filter through the ranks from the back. The defender's horses had not been trained for battle: they were used to being ridden to the fight and then being led back to a place of safety. When they found themselves surrounded by clinking armour and the press of troops they began to panic. The roar of the Welsh army, packed just in front of them, unsettled them further. Some froze, breaking the army's formation. Others turned and galloped away. Gruffydd saw his chance: he ordered his men forward, and the upheaval turned

EDWARD THE CONFESSOR

A coin of Edward the Confessor, who sent his nephew, the Earl of Hereford, to conquer Herefordshire.

into a rout. An estimated 500 Hereford men were slaughtered. Ralph, seeing no value in dying in a lost battle, turned his horse around and, ordering his men with him, headed for the only safety left to him: the castle of Hereford. For this reason he would forever be known in history as 'Ralph the Timid'. The army of the Welsh then turned for the city, and the sack of Hereford began.

Some of the militia did their duty. They armed themselves and ran to the town defences. But on the west side, where the Welsh were approaching, they were in a poor state. The last few years had been good to Hereford, a time of peace and prosperity. Why bother maintaining the walls? They only interfered with trade and cost money to repair. So the ditch was filled with rubbish, and the timber walls were left to rot. They did not delay the Welsh for long. Some people ran to the castle, but the great oak doors were bolted shut and no pleading would make them open. Inside lay Ralph, on his bed, deaf to the shouts and screams outside.

Others ran to the wooden cathedral, smoke from their burning homes in their nostrils. But that too would provide no sanctuary, for that was also where the treasures of Hereford were stored. It was where the Welsh were heading.

In charge of the cathedral was a man called Tremerig, a Welsh bishop more used to a wandering life than having care of a diocese. But his friend Athelstan, Bishop of Hereford, had been ill and had asked Tremerig to look after his duties. Now he found himself in the crowded cathedral, the normally quiet place filled with crying and shouting. He collected the canons and, with the great gold processional cross before him, marched out of the cathedral to order peace. The sight cowed the Welsh but the Danes, more recent converts, took more interest in the rich vestments they were wearing. The men were put to the sword. Tremerig's life was only saved by Gruffydd holding him close, though the old man fought and cursed him. A few of the canons tried to bar the great west door of the cathedral, but they too were quickly cut down. Now a second slaughter began. The raiders were desperate to find the gold and silver communion vessels, the books inlaid with jewels and ivory. In their search they destroyed the shrine of St Aethelbert, scattering his bones (although some say a young priest managed to escape with the saint's head).

Soon a fire broke out and the great wooden building that Athelstan had only recently built to the glory of God was burnt to ashes. Before Christmas, Tremerig was dead, his heart heavy with failure, as was Bishop Athelstan, who, when the news of the destruction of his cathedral was brought to him, never spoke again.

Fearful that Edward would send an avenging force when he heard of the sack of Hereford, Gruffydd ordered his men back over the border. And an avenging force did come, headed by Earl Harold Godwinnson, who pursued Gruffydd to his own hall of Rhuddlan, burning it to the ground.

Gruffydd fled to where he thought he would be safe: Dublin. But the Vikings had heard of Harold; they admired him. For a few days he was treated as an honoured guest while they decided what to do. Then he was dragged out to the sea shore, where his head was removed from his body with an axe. The head was sent to Harold who in turn took it to Edward. The Normans remembered this slight, ten years later, at Hastings.

THE NORMANS IN HEREFORDSHIRE

Normans did not arrive in Herefordshire in 1066, but had been playing a major part in the politics of the county for some twenty years before.

Hereford Cathedral Close, site of the confrontation between the King and the bishop. (David Phelps)

Edward, son of Aethelred the Unready, had found refuge in Normandy when his father was deposed by the Danish Swein Forkbeard and his mother married Forkbeard's son, Cnut. Edward spent over twenty years in exile and, by the time he returned in 1035, was more Norman than English.

There was a great deal of resentment among the English nobles at the number of Normans who came over with Edward. The anger coalesced around Earl Godwin, most powerful of the Saxons, a man Edward loathed but who was too powerful to move against.

Then Godwin's son, Swein, Earl of Hereford, went too far. He abducted the pretty young abbess of Leominster, not only to keep his bed warm at night but also to use the abbey lands to pay his

men. Edward, a religious man, reacted furiously, demanding the return of the abbess. Swein, he declared, must leave England by the next full moon, otherwise he would be declared a 'wolf's head', a person whom any man could kill with impunity.

Swein had no option but to comply. He was replaced as earl by Edward's nephew, Ralph of Mantes. Ralph set about defending the county in the Norman fashion, by building castles. Of five castles in this country built before 1066, four of them are in Herefordshire, at Burghill, Ewyas Harold, Hereford and Richard's Castle. These were not the mighty stone fortresses of later development, but wooden palisades enclosing a man-made mound, on which was a wooden fort whose defenders could see far over the surrounding countryside.

After the debacle of the Battle of Hereford, Edward had no choice but to appoint another of Godwin's sons, Harold, to the earldom. Harold set about improving the defences of Hereford and attacking the Welsh, eventually forcing a peace treaty on them, which was negotiated at Billingsley, near Bolstone.

After Harold's defeat at Hastings, local resistance to the Normans was led by Edric the Wild, a lord with land in North Herefordshire and Shropshire. Edric, together with opportunist Welsh, laid waste to much of north-west Herefordshire. So fierce was he that later legend describes him leading the 'Wild Hunt' – hunting souls for hell. By the time of the Domesday Book, 1086, only two Saxon names remained among the major landholders of Herefordshire.

AD 1139

THE SIEGE OF HEREFORD CASTLE

CIVIL WARS ARE often the worst kind of war. So it was for the dispute that broke out after the death of Henry I, William the Conqueror's son. Some of the deeds committed at the time were so awful that people said Christ and his saints slept.

Who was to blame? Many said it was the fault of Henry, who had died without a legitimate male heir (he had plenty of the illegitimate kind), so was forced to pass the crown to his daughter, Matilda. But, when Henry died, Matilda had three things acting against her: she was a woman, she was pregnant and, worse, she was in France, so Henry's nephew, Stephen, seized the Treasury and declared himself the rightful King.

Others said it was not really Henry's fault because his rightful heir, his son, the Young Henry, had drowned aboard the *White Ship*. He could have escaped but insisted his rescue boat go back to save his sister. The boat was overloaded with desperate people, capsized and everyone drowned (save the ship's baker, who got to land floating on a barrel).

Others said even that was still King Henry's fault, because he was under a curse. He had murdered his older brother, William Rufus, to get to the throne and kept his other brother Robert in a dungeon until he died.

Whatever the truth of it, the armies of Stephen and Matilda continually clashed for nineteen terrible years. Hereford Castle was controlled by soldiers loyal to King Stephen. Geoffrey Talbot was lord of Weobley; he had been Stephen's man but saw there were richer pickings to be had by going over to Matilda's camp. He and Milo of Gloucester laid siege to Hereford, hoping they would increase their fortunes.

There were too few men in the garrison to protect the whole length of the castle's wooden walls, so they retreated to the inner bailey, while Milo and Geoffrey made their base in the cathedral. Its stone walls were a good place to keep their men and their horses dry and warm.

So the siege continued. Matilda's men placed a trebuchet on one of the towers above the chancel of the cathedral to rain stones at the castle, to keep the defenders'

King Stephen, whose men held Hereford Castle.

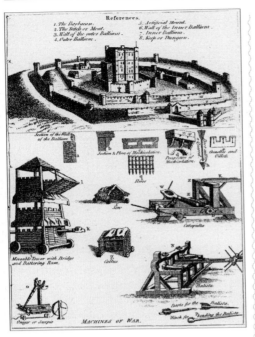

Siege engines of the era. (www.fromoldbooks.org)

Good managers always like to encourage employee suggestions, so the man was rewarded with a few coins and the defenders found themselves being pelted with rotting corpses.

They knew that there was no hope of rescue and surrendered the castle before too many grudges had been built up by Matilda's men. Geoffrey and Milo were richly rewarded, Milo becoming the new Earl of Hereford. Within a couple of years, however, they were both dead, Geoffrey killed in a pointless skirmish near Bath, Milo by a hunting accident in the Forest of Dean.

THE HEREFORDSHIRE SCHOOL

About the only good thing the Normans brought to Herefordshire (unless you like rabbits) was the building of a series of magnificent churches in what architectural historians describe as the Herefordshire School of Romanesque Sculpture.

Marcher lords had to do some pretty dreadful things, so it was natural that they looked for some eternal insurance through the building of churches. Fortunately they chose artistic geniuses to carry out the work, who were able to blend Norman figures, Saxon animals and Celtic abstract patterns. Two master masons have been identified, an expressive 'Chief Master' and a more subtle 'Aston Master'.

Churches in this style can be seen at Brinsop, Castle Frome, Eardisley, Fownhope, Leominster Priory and Rowlstone, but the masterpiece is at Kilpeck, built under the patronage of Hugh de Kilpeck. Famously it boasts some very graphic corbels, including a sheela-na-gig, a young lady being rather immodest with her private parts. These were once assumed to be fertility symbols

attention, but they had no intention of making a direct assault. That would cost too many men.

Geoffrey and Milo ordered their men to construct earthworks up to the palisade of the castle and then tunnels under it, shored up with great wood pillars under which firewood would be placed and set fire to, so bringing the tunnel – and the wall above it – crashing down.

Their excavations took them right through the graveyard, past numberless rotting corpses. They were under orders and also dodging the occasional arrow from the castle so, when they came to a body, it was thrown onto the pile of earth that was forming the rampart. Then some keen soldier suggested that some of the fresher ones, still intact enough to make the journey, should be taken up the cathedral tower and catapulted over the castle walls: a little disease can shorten a siege considerably.

Above *Corbels, Kilpeck Church. (David Phelps)*

Right *South door of Kilpeck Church. (David Phelps)*

but historians now think they were warnings to young people of the dangers of the flesh. Not all such sculptures survived. Andrew Haggard, visiting in the twenties, found one of the corbels recently damaged. A local man described to him what happened: 'Ah, that wur Miss ---. A never could suffer that un, so a got her a pole and a pothered un off.'

At Shobdon, north-west Herefordshire, there was said to have been an even better example of the school, built by Oliver de Merimond, but this was shamefully pulled down by Lord Bateman in 1752 and re-assembled as a folly on top of a nearby hill, where the sculpture is now badly weather-beaten.

FAIR ROSAMUND

EVENTUALLY EVEN THE barons became tired of the killing and longed for order. It was agreed that, on Stephen's death, Matilda's son Henry should become king. This duly happened in 1154.

Unlike his predecessor, Henry II was a charismatic leader and a skilled politician. He gave his nobles just enough warfare that they had a chance of getting rich and head-hunted clerics who would be good administrators. Before he even came to the throne he had enchanted the King of France's wife Eleanor of Aquitaine, so much so that she had obtained a divorce and married Henry. With her lands he was one of the richest men in Christendom.

By 1163 Henry had turned his thoughts to the perennial problem of Wales. The Lord Rhys had become too powerful, controlling both north and south of the country. On his way into Wales, Henry stayed at Clifford Castle – where he was once again captivated by a woman, this time the teenage Rosamund, daughter of Walter Clifford.

Although the nephew of Milo of Gloucester, mentioned above, Walter had started out as a mere steward of the de Tosny family, who owned Clifford Castle. It was they who transformed a small motte-and-bailey castle into a formidable stone fortress the ruins of which we can see today. Then he married into the family and started calling himself Walter Clifford. After the civil war he refused to give the castle back to its rightful owners. The actions of his daughter would ensure that he never had to.

Henry persuaded her father that Rosamund should join the court. By 1166 Eleanor was pregnant with the future King John. Henry turned to the beautiful Rosamund for solace whilst his wife was indisposed carrying and giving birth to his child. A strange idea grew up in later centuries that Henry had built a labyrinth for Rosamund, on the site of Blenheim Palace, to hide her from his queen. This is unlikely as, in those days, the court was constantly travelling, as affairs of state and chances to go hunting dictated. It would mean Rosamund and Henry would rarely see each other. More likely Rosamund travelled with the court, whatever Eleanor thought about it. Certainly, after John, she and Henry had no more children.

The affair, which must have been well known within court circles, became public knowledge in 1174. Royal mistresses are not unknown: in fact, monarchs who do not have them are far fewer than those that do. However, in 1176,

Tomb of Eleanor of Aquitaine and Henry II at Fontevraud. (Elanor Gamgee)

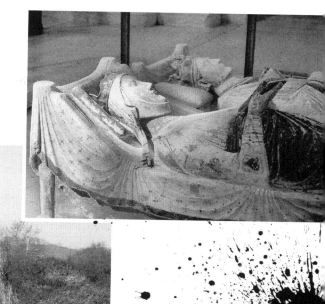

Clifford Castle. (David Phelps)

Rosamund fell ill and retired to a nunnery at Godstow in Oxfordshire, where she died soon afterwards. The belief that she was poisoned by Eleanor is, again, a later addition to her story, with no contemporary backing – although one report of the 1630s has it that her original tombstone was decorated with an image of a cup of poison.

Both Henry and her father endowed the nunnery with land and a magnificent tomb that became something of a shrine for the local people. After Henry's death it was visited by the Bishop of Lincoln, who was scandalised to see it covered by roses and candles as if it was the tomb of a saint and worried what message that would send to women. He ordered it destroyed and the body re-buried among the common people with these words on the grave marker: 'Here in the tomb lies the rose of the world, not a pure rose; she who used to smell sweet still smells – but not sweet.'

To spite the bishop the nuns put Rosamund's bones in a perfumed leather bag. At the Dissolution of the Monasteries this tomb was opened. According to Leland (or Leyland, an antiquarian appointed by Henry VIII and charged with travelling the country recording the effects of the Dissolution) the scent of roses still remained: 'Her bones were closyd in lede, and withyn that, bones were closyd in letter. When it was openid there was a very swete smell came out of it.'

Rosamund's death is commemorated at Hereford Cathedral each year on 6 July.

WALTER MAPP

Born into a land-holding family from Wormsley, Walter had a glittering career in the Church and the diplomatic service, becoming a close friend of Henry II. He held many senior clerical posts, many at the same time, including being a canon of Hereford Cathedral. In 1199 he was a candidate to become Bishop of Hereford but was passed over. It was he who possibly introduced the King to Rosamund Clifford.

But it is for his collection *De Nugis Curialium* (Of the Trifles of Courtiers) that he is best remembered. Full of anecdotes and trivia written in a satirical vein, it includes the first mention of a vampire in Britain, as well as attacks on clerical abuse. He is especially hard on the Cistercian order, normally viewed as exemplary ascetics but whom Walter considers drunken louts. There is evidence that he introduced the disruptive character of Lancelot into the Arthurian circle.

Some idea of his wit can be found in this translation of his 'Drinking Song':

I propose to end my days in a tavern drinking,
May some Christian hold for me the glass while I am shrinking;
That the cherubim may cry, when they see me sinking,
God be gracious to a soul of this man's way of thinking.

A glass of wine amazingly enlightens one's internals,
'Tis wings bedewed with nectar that fly up to the eternals,
Bottles cracked in taverns have much the sweeter kernels,
Than the sups allowed to us in the College journals.

Appropriately for such a satirist, he is commemorated annually at Hereford Cathedral every 1 April.

AD 1240

PETER D'AQUABLANCA

IF WE ARE to believe the monk chroniclers, King John was the worst monarch to sit on the English throne. He certainly made the mistake of upsetting the Marcher lords, who met at Barons' Cross near Leominster to decide on a curb to the King's powers that would eventually become the Magna Carta. The other thing that John did wrong was dying while his son, Henry III, was only a child. It meant the boy had to rely on those who surrounded him to run the kingdom. Inevitably this made nobles who were not close to the King jealous, thinking they could do a better job.

Things became worse when Henry III married Eleanor of Provence, who brought hordes of her fellow countrymen with her, all looking for rich pickings. One of these was Peter d'Aquablanca who, though only ordained a few months before, was made Bishop of Hereford.

Peter was a career diplomat, so he was not going to spend much of his time in Hereford. Instead, he appointed a relation called Bernard to perform all the tedious Church stuff. Worse than that, Peter picked more of his relations to fill other lucrative posts, which the local clergy thought they should have been given. When Peter was in the diocese he did not make himself popular, taking back land into his own control that his predecessors had given away. This was a time of tension between the Church and the townspeople, the Church insisting that all the dead should be buried in the cathedral graveyard and pay large amounts for the privilege. They also tried to prevent Hereford market spreading onto Church property, which the tradespeople greatly resented as it prevented them making a living. Peter refused to negotiate and, no other resolution seeming likely, a group from the town burst into the cathedral, caught the unfortunate Bernard in the nave, chased him into a side chapel and clubbed him to death. Peter was absent, being treated at Montpelier for his obesity and gout.

But Henry valued Peter for one specific skill, that of making money, even if not honestly. The bishop, on the King's authority, ordered the other bishops to affix their seals on

Henry III.

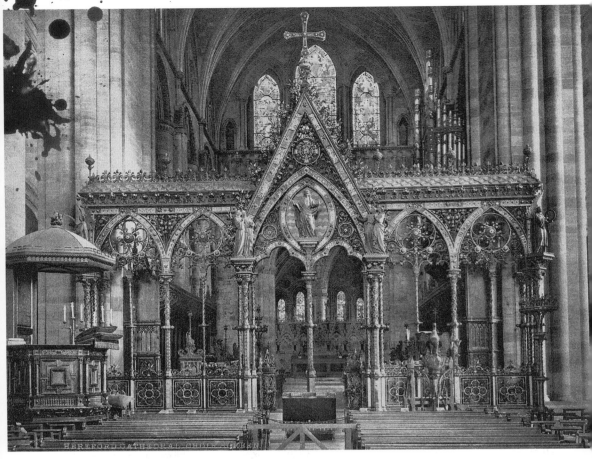

Hereford Cathedral, where Peter's relative, Bernard, was beaten to death. (LC-DIG-ppmsc-08439)

blank documents which, Peter assured them, would only be used for some trifling purpose. In fact they were filled in and sent to the Pope. Each piece of paper now claimed to be a bond for a large sum of money. On this security the Pope lent King Henry enormous sums. However, when the Pope sent a legate to the bishops asking for repayment of these completely fictitious loans, there was understandable outrage from the bishops. Many clergy found themselves having to pay a tenth of their income to pay for the loan, with severe penalties for those who failed. One contemporary chronicler describes this

as 'the shepherd and the wolf combining to lay waste the flock'. Peter also collected money for a crusade, although the money went only into the King's coffers. Such actions would make even an investment banker go pale.

But Henry had antagonised some of the powerful Marcher lords who, allied to Simon de Montfort, played their trump card, allying with their erstwhile enemies, the Welsh. A combined force ravaged western Herefordshire, stealing livestock and burning crops and homesteads.

When King Henry came to Hereford to deal with the lords, he was incensed to find neither bishop, dean, canons nor any other member of the clergy in the cathedral to perform their duties. Peter was ordered back to Hereford – and that proved his undoing.

One of de Montfort's supporters, Walter de Baskerville, attacked Hereford Cathedral, dragged the screaming Peter from his own altar and imprisoned him and several of the canons, who just happened to be Peter's nephews, in his castle at Eardisley. After two year's incarceration Peter was released, but his health seems to have been broken by the experience. Even though the King's party was eventually victorious, Henry seems to have decided to keep much of the bishop's lands rather than return them. Peter died within three months of his release. He was not mourned.

The people of Hereford can still see his most lasting monument, the magnificent North Transept of the cathedral. As they marvel at it they might like to contemplate that it was paid for by fines imposed by Peter on their ancestors.

MARCHER LORDS

As we have seen, it was immensely difficult for English kings to keep the Welsh their side of the border. It was also intensely annoying that the Welsh should keep their own laws and customs and not defer to their mighty neighbours. To William the Bastard it was soon clear that keeping the Welsh was going to be time-consuming and expensive so he hit upon a novel solution: he privatised the problem.

He chose 150 of his most trusted supporters and told them that, if they accepted land along the Welsh border, they could do virtually what they liked there, as long as they kept the Welsh out of England. They could build castles where they liked, without asking his permission

and, if they felt like going into Welsh territory and carving out more land for themselves – well, he was not going to stop them.

Like all privatisations it proved a mixed blessing. Yes, they did keep the Welsh more or less under control and English rule gradually extended further and further into Wales, but, in effect, he had created 150 petty kingdoms, including the three mighty earldoms of Hereford, Shrewsbury and Chester. Often they were not content to fight the Welsh, but regularly turned on each other. Over time they inter-bred with the Welsh nobility, so that Marcher/Welsh pacts became more likely. Worse, they resented any interference from the Crown but regularly used their power to interfere in the running of the kingdom. Many later kings must have bitterly regretted William's solution.

Typical of the breed was William de Braose, Lord of Bramber. In 1175 he invited three Welsh princes, including Seisyll ap Dyfnwal, and many other nobles, to a Christmas feast at Abergavenny Castle, to discuss peace. But William blamed Seisyll for the death of his uncle. When the guests had disarmed and entered the hall they were set upon by William's men and killed. Then William hunted down Seisyll's only remaining son, Cadwaladr, a boy of seven, and murdered him. Understandably he is known in the area as the Ogre of Abergavenny.

His wife, Maud de St Valery, was also a force to be reckoned with. In 1198 she held the castle of Painscastle against a vast Welsh army for three weeks, until reinforcements arrived. Legend said that she built Hay Castle single-handedly in one night, carrying the stones in her apron. By the name Moll Wallbe she was held up as a bogey-woman by generations of Welsh mothers, who threatened their children that she would come and get them if they were not good.

Hall of Abergavenny Castle, site of the 1175 massacre. (David Phelps)

Once a firm supporter of King John, William eventually fell out with the King over money. John asked William to send his eldest son to London as a hostage but Maud, knowing that John had killed Arthur of Brittany, a young boy who some thought had better claim to the throne than John's son, refused to send him. John sent an army to depose William, who fled to France as a beggar, dying a year later. Maud and her son were imprisoned in the dungeons of Corfe Castle, where they starved to death.

Her daughter founded the Hospital of St John at Aconbury in her memory, on land given her by King John. The Marcher lords, fearful at what had happened to William, forced John to limit his power by agreeing to the Magna Carta, clause 39 of which reads: 'no man shall be taken, imprisoned, outlawed, banished or in any way destroyed, nor will he be proceeded against or prosecuted, except by the lawful judgement of his peers or the law of the land.'

AD 1265

PRINCE EDWARD'S FLIGHT

PRINCE EDWARD WAS a very different man to his father, Henry III. Tall (he had acquired the nickname Longshanks by the time he became King Edward I in 1272) and charismatic, even in his late teens many thought he would be a better ruler than Henry.

He came to Hereford in less than ideal circumstances in 1264, however, after he was captured by Simon de Montfort, 6th Earl of Leicester, at the Battle of Lewes. *Grafton's Chronicle* describes the scene after the battle in graphic detail: 'Then was the field covered with dead bodyes, and gasping and groning was heard on every syde... Christian blood that day was shed without pitie!' Edward was taken to Hereford Castle under the guard of de Montfort's son, Henry.

Such was the importance of this hostage that Henry took it in turns with Thomas, Gilbert de Clare, the Earl of Gloucester's brother, to sleep in Edward's chamber, to make sure he did not escape.

Simon de Montfort hoped that he could eventually control Edward, so he was treated well. He was therefore allowed exercise, the most popular form for the nobility being riding. Under close escort, Edward was allowed small expeditions in the Haywood royal forest to the south of the city, or the open ground to the north

called the Widemarsh. He was also given his privacy – too much privacy. The Prince began to send secret messages to Roger Mortimer, a knight who had escaped

Edward I.

Below *Prince Edward runs down an enemy on horseback. It was this skill which would see him escape from captivity in Hereford.*

Right *Henry III captured at the Battle of Lewes. He handed over his son as a hostage.*

was beaten by Henry – well, you wouldn't give your captive the fastest mount, would you? After that he contented himself with cheering on the others. It came to the hour of vespers and Henry ordered a return to the castle. They all turned their horses' heads back to the city. Then, suddenly, Edward swung his mount and galloped for the trees. Angrily, the others chased after him, but their horses were tired from all the racing. Edward's horse, however, was still fresh. Edward reached one of Mortimer's supporters, Roger Croft, who was hidden in the trees and they rode off in the direction of Wigmore. Henry had lost his father's most valuable prize.

With the escape of Edward the royal cause was greatly strengthened. Edward organised an army to destroy Simon de Montfort and release his father, Henry III, who had also been captured at the Battle of Lewes. In desperation, Simon made a treaty with Llywelyn, Prince of Wales. But before the Welsh could cross the border, Edward's army had caught up with Simon at Evesham. The encounter that followed was 'a cruell and bloodye bataille'.

the Battle of Lewes and was now back at Wigmore. A bold plan to rescue the Prince was formed.

On 28 May, Prince Edward, Henry de Montfort and Thomas de Clare, as well as other lords of the rebel party, were exercising their horses at Widemarsh. The Prince suggested that the men race each other, an idea that was gladly taken up. Edward took part in the first race, when he

The royal army, an estimated 10,000 men, was twice the size of de Montfort's. As an almighty storm broke overhead, the battle quickly turned into a massacre. One of the first to die was Simon's own son, split open by a sword in sight of his father. Outnumbered, Simon's army fought to the last, until Simon was killed by a lance thrust from Roger Mortimer. His last words are said to have been: 'I yield to God alone, never to dogs and perjurers!' A few of de Montfort's men, including William de Baskerville, did manage to escape. The rest were slaughtered. Amidst the carnage, Simon's body was found. It was stripped and cut into pieces: 'Some malicious persons cut off his head, mutilating him otherwise with a barbaritie too disgusting to mention [the removal, allegedly, of his testicles]. His feet also, and his handes, were cut off from the body, and sent to sundrie places.'

Roger Mortimer sent the head to his own wife at Wigmore as a token of victory. One foot was sent to Llywelyn, to let him know he need not bother coming to Simon's aid. One hand was sent to de Montfort's widow, Eleanor, King Henry's own sister. The King himself was found, safe but bloodied, on the battlefield and restored to power, though it would not be many years before he died and Edward could at last sit on the throne he had done so much to maintain.

The ruins of Wigmore Castle, Herefordshire, once home of the Mortimers.

AD 1282

ST THOMAS CANTILUPE

THE PRIESTS OF Hereford Cathedral were worried. While other cathedrals had saints' relics that attracted pilgrims and money, Hereford had lost its relics in a Welsh raid. Little did they know that their current bishop would solve the problem...

Thomas Cantilupe's father had been a courtier of King John's and his great uncle was Bishop of Worcester, both of which were quite useful if you were going to end up Bishop of Hereford. His great uncle once asked him what he wanted to be when he grew up. 'A soldier,' replied the young boy. 'Then you shall be a soldier to serve the King of kings,' said the bishop, which might not have been what young Thomas intended.

But he was clever and rose rapidly through the ranks. Although he supported de Montfort, this did not prevent Edward I from offering him the see of Hereford, which Thomas accepted rather reluctantly. While he enjoyed disputing the finer points of theology, now he found himself up against Marcher lords who were more inclined to stick a dagger in you than compliment you on a fine point of rhetoric.

He fell out with Gilbert de Clare, Earl of Gloucester, when the latter encroached on the bishop's hunting territory in the Malverns. This was no mere dispute over recreation: the meat was needed to supply the bishop's household. A court case decided in the bishop's favour and the Red Earl's Dyke was dug to clearly mark their respective boundaries.

He fell out with Lord Clifford, who had stolen the bishop's cattle and beaten up some of his tenants. By way of penance Thomas forced the mighty lord to walk barefoot to the high altar of the cathedral while being followed by Thomas, who was hitting him with a stick.

Then he went too far and fell out with the Archbishop of Canterbury over money. In a fit of rage the archbishop excommunicated Thomas. The only way to solve that problem was to go to the Pope in Rome to get the excommunication lifted. This was done but, on the journey back, Thomas died. His chaplain, Richard Swinfield, boiled the body until the flesh came off the bones and returned with these to Hereford.

Swinfield, the new bishop, set about proving what a saintly man Thomas had been. When he died he had been wearing a hair shirt, which would constantly itch and prickle, to mortify his flesh. It was recalled that he would never allow his sister Julianna to kiss him. Then, after the bones were brought back, a miracle occurred: when Gilbert de Clare touched the casket

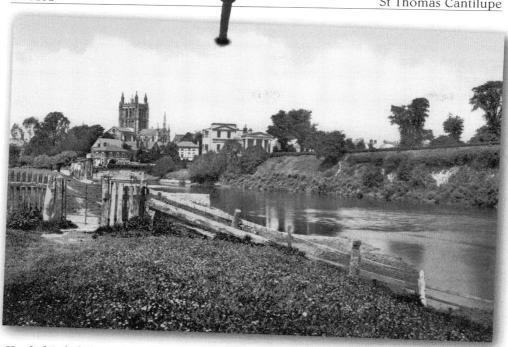

Hereford Cathedral, site of precious relics. (LC-DIG-ppmsc-08438)

in which the bones were contained, 'dry bones in his presence began to bleed afresh, and in such a quantity that he and all might see the cask in which they were carried, imbrued with the same'. This surprising event allegedly made the earl repent of all the mischief he had done to the Church.

Eventually a committee was set up to discuss Thomas' saintly qualities and thirty-eight alleged miracles were put before them. Edith Oldecriste, a mad woman of the town, was returned to sanity by praying to the saint. William the Scabby, a Welsh rebel, had to be hanged twice by Lord de Braose. The first time the gallows collapsed; during the second attempt, Lady de Braose prayed to the saint, promising Thomas a candle the height of William if the man was returned to life – which, a day after the execution, he was, William himself turning up to testify to the truth of it. A young boy, his head crushed by a wagon wheel, was restored to life on his mother praying to the saint. When, in Edward I's presence, the body of the saint was being transferred from the Lady Chapel to a new shrine, the ceremony went horribly wrong: even the strongest workmen could not lift the coffin, but two young boys, without sin, were able to lift it and carry it to the shrine with no effort. Bishop Swinfield himself said that he had derived great benefit from drinking water in which a bone of Thomas's had been dipped.

The committee agreed that Thomas should be declared a saint, but it was forty years before the Pope eventually agreed, there being some concern that Thomas had too close a link to the Templars, an organisation the Pope had recently disbanded, burning the leaders as heretics. Finally, in 1320, Thomas became the last Englishman to be canonized before the Reformation. Sadly, Bishop Swinfield had died four years before.

AD 1317

THE HIDEOUS DEATH OF HUGH DESPENSER

EDWARD II WAS a very unpopular King – so unpopular, in fact, that in 1327 he was deposed by his own wife, Isabella of France, who was angered by – amongst other things – his fondness for one Hugh Despenser the Younger, 1st Lord Despenser. The final straw came when Edward took away her estates, only giving her an allowance of twenty shillings a day – and that often late paid. Isabella fled to France and joined forces with Roger Mortimer, 1st Earl of March. They soon became partners, in the modern sense of the word as well as in the sense that they were united in their plan to depose Edward. When they landed in Suffolk they found every important lord rallying to their cause. The King and Lord Despenser fled to Wales but were captured and taken to Hereford. Despite Hugh's desperate attempts to starve himself to death before the terrible fate he knew awaited him, he was brought to trial before

Edward II.

Isabella and Mortimer at Hereford Castle. Unsurprisingly he was found guilty of treason and sentenced to be hanged, drawn and quartered. As if that was not enough, he was also sentenced to be disembowelled for his crimes against the Queen.

Immediately after sentencing Despenser was dressed in a shroud on which were written the words of a penitential psalm, tied to a hurdle and dragged to High Town by four horses. Here a great fire had been lit and a great crowd had assembled to see the fun. He was stripped and hanged on a gallows 50ft high. But before he could choke to death he was cut down and tied to a ladder so that the crowd would have a good view of what happened next.

He was castrated and his genitals thrown into the fire. He was still conscious and forced to watch. When his entrails were slowly pulled out he let out a ghastly, inhuman howl, much to the merriment of the crowd. Finally his heart was cut out and also thrown into the fire.

After being cut down he was beheaded and his body cut into four pieces. The head was sent to London, to be stuck on Tower Bridge. Mortimer and Isabella are reported to have feasted with their supporters while they watched.

When Edward III had become King Despenser's wife begged that what

Execution of Hugh Despenser – although Hereford has never looked so palatial.

remained of his body be returned to her for a decent burial, but by that time only the skull, a thigh bone and some vertebrae could be found.

In 2008 a part skeleton was found at Hulton Abbey in Shropshire. It bore the marks of ritual murder similar to Despenser's end and was missing those parts that had been returned to his wife. Carbon dating linked it to the fourteenth century and it was the skeleton of a man aged roughly forty, the age Despenser was when he died. At the time the area was in the possession of Despenser's brother-in-law. Perhaps his last resting place had been discovered?

Edward II was imprisoned in various castles in the country, eventually ending up at Berkeley in Gloucestershire.

Roger had a problem as to what to do with him. If he remained alive he was a constant threat, but, if he died, his body must be exhibited. Any marks of violence and Roger would be blamed. An ingenious solution was found: according to some, through the intervention of the Bishop of Hereford, Edward was thrown over a table, his breeches pulled down and he was impaled with a red-hot poker. It is said that, on a quiet night, his screams can still be heard ringing through the castle.

THE BATTLING BISHOP OF HEREFORD!

Adam of Orleton was a clever young man, who had the luck to catch the eye of Edmund Mortimer, the powerful lord of Wigmore, who paid for him to receive the best education (which was in Paris at the time) and rise quickly in the Church, eventually becoming Bishop of Hereford.

Edward II did not care for clever and sober clerics around him, preferring ones who could tell a good story and hold their wine, so Adam spent much of his early career at the Papal Court in Avignon, negotiating the canonization of Thomas Cantilupe. He became a favourite of the Pope, John XXII, and assisted in the prosecution of the Knights Templar, accusing them of various unnatural crimes, including sodomy – a charge which might, some think, have inspired him to suggest the horrible method of murdering the King.

Eventually, in 1317, the Pope appointed him Bishop of Hereford, much against Edward's wishes. By this time Roger Mortimer had succeeded his father as lord of Wigmore. He must have known Adam since childhood and retained his friendship. When Roger and the Marcher lords rebelled against the King, Adam provided some of his own men for Roger's cause, but the Marcher lords were defeated at the Battle of Boroughbridge, many executed and Roger imprisoned in the Tower of London.

King Edward arrested Adam for high treason, the first time a senior cleric had faced such a charge. Adam refused to plead, claiming clerical immunity. His trial was interrupted by a great horde of clergy bursting through the doors, headed by no less than three archbishops and ten bishops, their crosses held in front of them, who led Adam away to safety.

Edward sent his men to Hereford to seize the bishop's goods, although his friends managed to hide much of them before they arrived. The Prior of St Guthlac in Ross, who had assisted the King's men, was set upon by Adam's supporters and almost killed. But Adam was reduced to the status almost of an outlaw. The man who was wont to travel with a train of forty horses was now forced to travel on foot, with barely any man prepared to sell him bread or give him a roof.

Then, after two year's confinement, Roger Mortimer escaped from the Tower by drugging his guards and managed to reach the safety of France. Edward suspected Bishop Adam was behind the planning of the escape but could not prove it. Adam was also close to the Queen, and suggested she go to France to join forces with Mortimer.

King Edward II's son, Edward III, was only fourteen, so a Council of Regency was appointed, including Adam. Edward bided his time. The other Marcher lords increasingly resented Roger, especially when he appointed himself Earl of March, in effect ruler of Wales. Three years after his father's death, Edward acted, seizing Roger, accusing him of high treason and ordering him to be hanged, drawn and quartered.

However Edward seems to have borne Adam no ill will, for he ended his days as Bishop of Winchester.

AD 1349

THE BLACK DEATH

IN 1349 THE first thing the people of Hereford would have known of the coming horror was news of many deaths in the port of Bristol. They kept calm and prayed that it would stay there. They were not going to be so lucky.

What became known as the Great Pestilence probably started in China and travelled along the Silk Road to the Middle East and then Europe, carried by fleas on the then-common black rat. It killed between 30 and 60 per cent of humanity.

Death comes for the great and good of Hereford. (With kind permission of the Thomas Fisher Rare Book Library, University of Toronto)

'Dance of Death' by Hans Holbein, a popular motif after the horror of the Black Death.

The symptoms were unmistakeable. Buboes or tumours would appear in the groin, neck or armpit, which oozed pus and blood. The victim would suffer from acute fever and start vomiting blood. Then death would be almost inevitable, within two to seven days.

The actual effect on Hereford was undocumented, but we do know that, of 500 clergy in the county at the time, about 200 died. In 1993, while building the new Mappa Mundi building, a plague pit was discovered, containing about 400 bodies.

They had not been thrown in haphazardly, the way you see in films, but laid carefully side by side, which seems to indicate that some form of funeral service was still provided them. Then a layer of earth was thrown over the bodies to protect against infection and stench, to await the next collection of bodies.

People were unclear about the causes but it was understood that close contact with a potential victim was not a good idea. Farmers were unwilling to come to the city, so to prevent the people of Hereford starving to death the market was moved to the Whitecross, thoughtfully provided by Bishop Charleton some ten years before. Here country people could leave their produce to be collected by the townspeople, who paid by dropping coins into a pot of vinegar.

The plague proved not to be a one-off event but returned in 1361 and other occasions right up to the seventeenth century, although not with such virulence, perhaps because of increased immunity. Society came close to breakdown, with complaints of an increase in marauders and criminals roaming the countryside; those peasants who had survived were no longer prepared to put up with pre-plague conditions, which would lead to a great deal of social unrest in the years to come.

AD 1417

SIR JOHN OLDCASTLE

THE **OLDCASTLES WERE** an old Herefordshire family, holding land around Almeley. They were well-connected: Oldcastles served as sheriffs and represented the county in Parliament throughout the fourteenth century.

Sir John was involved in the campaign against Owen Glyndwr in 1401, having charge of the castles at Builth and then Kidwelly. During this time he became friendly with Henry, Prince of Wales. In 1409 his fortunes improved even more when he married Joan de la Pole, Lady Cobham, his third marriage and her fourth. Henceforth he could call himself 'Lord Cobham'.

Herefordshire was a hot-bed of Lollardry – which held that several key Catholic doctrines, including transubstantiation, were false – and Sir John shared these beliefs. However, any accusations of heresy or of supporting unlicensed preachers were dismissed because of his friendship with Henry V. But then a search for heretical books – which were to be burnt – uncovered some belonging to Sir John. He was summoned to a meeting with the King and the bishops. Henry prevented the bishops from taking any action against his old friend, asking him to recant – but instead, Sir John fled. Henry therefore allowed Sir John's excommunication.

Sir John was arrested and brought to the Tower, where he maintained he was a true Christian but believed putting one's faith in images was nothing more than idolatry and that undertaking pilgrimages and confessing to a priest had no effect on the soul. This was enough to condemn him. Henry granted him a respite of forty days and during this time, with the help of a fellow Lollard, a parchment maker, he escaped.

The Lollards of England rose in his defence and a mob gathered, which planned to capture the King at his palace in Eltham during Twelfth Night festivities and set up a commonwealth, but the plot was discovered, the mob dispersed and Oldcastle fled to Herefordshire.

He evaded capture for four years, hiding in the Olchon Valley. Perhaps he met his old enemy Owen Glyndwr on one of his wanderings, as he was also a refugee in this area. In his absence he was accused of masterminding various plots against the King, including encouraging a Scottish invasion while the King was in France, fighting the Agincourt campaign.

In November 1417 his hiding place was discovered, a farmhouse in the valley that still exists. Hearing the soldiers at the door Oldcastle jumped out of a bedroom window, badly injuring his foot. Despite his injuries Sir John fought his attackers for some time before being overpowered and chained.

He was taken to London, carried on a horse litter. He was condemned as a traitor and heretic by Parliament without need for further defence. On Christmas Day, despite his injuries, he was dragged on a hurdle through the streets to a specially built gallows where he was hanged in chains above a bonfire until his body, and the gallows, were burnt to ashes.

Because of his friendship with the King it is often assumed that he was the basis for Shakespeare's *Sir John Falstaff*. Indeed, in the original production of Henry VI, Part I, the character was called Oldcastle, but was changed in deference to the then Lord Cobham. He also appears in *Foxe's Book of Martyrs*.

LOLLARDRY

As the Church became more powerful it became more corrupt. When Adam of Orleton, on being appointed Bishop of Hereford, set about visiting his diocese he found in many parishes that the rectors

The Olchon Valley, where Sir John Oldcastle evaded capture for four years. (David Phelps)

Execution of Sir John Oldcastle.

were non-resident. Things were worse at Wigmore Abbey. The refectory was open all hours and to all comers: members of the convent and their friends came to carouse at any hour they chose and, after grumbling about the food, they would go to the monks' cells to drink. Women frequented the abbey and joined in the revels. Mass was not celebrated and, instead of silence, shameful oaths could be heard everywhere.

William Langland, the author of *Piers Plowman*, composed on the Malvern Hills, used much of his prose to satirize clerics

and his words in turn inspired John Ball, one of the leaders of the Peasants' Revolt of 1381.

Anti-clerical opinion culminated with John Wycliffe and his followers, the Lollards. They were given that name, which was originally a term of abuse, from their habit of quiet singing, the word being close in derivation to a lullaby. Wycliffe denied that Christ was physically present at the Mass and stressed the importance of preaching and studying scripture rather than relying on priests. He therefore set about the first complete English translation of the Bible. The man he got to translate the Old Testament was Nicholas Hereford, from an old established family from the Mordiford area. It is tempting to hold Nicholas responsible for the 'Cider Bible', a copy of Wycliffe's bible that translates part of Matthew's gospel, 'For he shall be great in the sight of the Lord and shall drink neither wine nor cider.' This can be found in the Chained Library of Hereford Cathedral, the largest collection of pre AD 1500 books in the world.

With the death of Sir John Oldcastle Lollardism ceased to be a political force, although the bishops of Hereford still had their work cut out hunting for signs of it and forcing people to recant for the next fifty years.

AD 1461

THE BATTLE OF
MORTIMER'S CROSS

WHEN HENRY V died of dysentry in 1415 his son, now Henry VI, was only nine months old. As we have seen before, it was bad luck for a nation to have a child as king. In Henry's case it was even worse. As he grew it became clear that the lad was dim-witted, ill-suited to being the divinely appointed ruler.

Worse than that, he married Margaret of France, whom many at court regarded as mad – although no one was sure if that was her general disposition or if she had been driven to distraction by the actions of her husband. Naturally there were those who thought they could do a better job, most notably Richard, Duke of York.

By 1455 the dispute had degenerated into civil war, which became known as the War of the Roses (although not until the nineteenth century). Who you supported depended not on your own inclination, but whom your over-lord supported. Because the Duke of York controlled large estates on the Welsh border, most knights in Herefordshire supported the Yorkist cause.

But things did not go well for the Yorkists. On 31 December 1460 they were heavily defeated at the Battle of Wakefield and the Duke of York killed. His heir, Edward, Earl of March, had spent Christmas in Shrewsbury. Although only eighteen, he was tall, strong and athletic.

When he heard the news of his father's defeat and death his immediate impulse was to head for his supporters in London, but then he was informed that a large Lancastrian army led by Jasper Tudor, Earl of Pembroke, was coming from South Wales to join up with Margaret's victorious army. He knew that, if they came together, his cause was doomed.

Edward had been brought up at the mighty Mortimer Castle of Wigmore so that is where he now went. It was an area he knew well and where he had many allies, including Sir Richard Croft of Croft Castle, who could advise him on tactics.

Gradually Edward assembled a force of about 4,000 men, while Jasper was collecting a force of 5,000 Welsh, English and foreign mercenaries. This took some time and it was only in late January that he was ready to march. Given the winter season, he was forced to take the Brecon road rather than the more direct but higher Builth road. When Edward heard this he could plan where best to meet him – and he chose Mortimer's Cross.

On the day before the battle, Candlemas Day, about noon, three suns had been seen in the sky. Some of Edward's troops were aghast, but Edward let it be known that this was a good sign, a sign of the Trinity, showing that God was on their side. From

The battlefield, with the high ground held by the Yorkist forces. (David Phelps)

that moment he took as his banner the Sun in Splendour. Meteorologists call this phenomenon a parhelion; it is caused by ice crystals refracting light.

The following day the Lancastrian troops approached from the south. They would have seen that the Yorkists held the advantage of the high ground. On Sir Richard Croft's advice, Edward waited for the enemy to make the first move. Leaving their baggage train near where the monument to the battle now stands,the Lancastrians went forward. The attack was met by a withering storm of arrows. Despite this, the attack on Edward's right flank was successful and the wing was pushed back. It then broke. Owen Tudor, Jasper's father, now attacked Edward's left flank, seeking to encircle the enemy, but this force was routed. Edward, holding the centre, repulsed an attack by Jasper. Then he drove the Lancastrians back to the Lugg, where they were massacred or drowned. It is estimated that 4,000 men died that day, mostly Lancastrians. In a medieval battle most of the killing happened when one side realised it had lost and turned and tried to flee. Near Kinsham there is a place called Slaughterhouse Covert which is where, perhaps, many Lancastrians met their fate – or at least the poor ones. It was the custom in those days that those of the knightly class should not be butchered on the battlefield, but captured alive, for later ransom. But

this was a civil war, and there were scores to settle and revenge to be taken.

Jasper Tudor had managed to evade capture, but his father Owen Tudor was not so lucky. He had earned special enmity for marrying the widow of Henry V. He was dragged to the block set up in High Town in Hereford by Roger Vaughan, one of Edward's most trusted Herefordshire supporters.

Even as he was being dragged into the square he refused to believe that such an important captive would be summarily executed. It was only when the collar of his doublet was ripped off by the executioner so that the axe could cut more cleanly that he accepted his fate: 'The head that was wont to lie in Queen Catherine's lap will soon lie in a basket,' he is reported to have said as he was forced to kneel.

After his beheading a mad woman claimed the head, washed it and placed it on the market cross, surrounded by over 100 candles. Jasper had his revenge on Roger and his half-brother, Thomas Vaughan of Hergest, ten years later, at the Battle of Banbury.

Edward moved north and defeated Margaret's forces at the Battle of Towton. King Edward, the fourth of that name, a Herefordshire man, had become King of England. But he would die young, leaving a child as heir, with tragic consequences and the return of the Tudors.

Edward V, son of Edward IV. He famously vanished in the Tower. (With kind permission of the Thomas Fisher Rare Book Library, University of Toronto)

THE COUNCIL OF THE MARCHES

What we know as the War of the Roses has been described by some historians as a war between the Marcher lords. By the end of it they had been bled white, many families utterly destroyed and their power broken.

By way of replacement, Edward IV set up the Council of the Marches and Wales, based in Ludlow Castle, in 1472, to rule on behalf of his infant son, the future Edward V. As well as the Welsh principality it had jurisdiction over Cheshire, Shropshire, Herefordshire, Worcestershire and Gloucestershire.

After his father's death in 1483, Edward V quickly disappeared, under still mysterious circumstances. In 1485, Henry Tudor became King after killing Edward's uncle Richard III at the Battle of Bosworth Field. Henry kept the Council, now made up of a president and twenty

members of the great and the good of the border. Eventually Cheshire succeeded in separating itself from the Council and becoming part of the rest of England. Worcestershire tried but was unsuccessful. The other three counties seem to have been quite happy with the rule of the Council.

By the end of the sixteenth century it had become an admired experiment in regional government. Its jurisdiction was 'such causes and matters as be or hencetofore hath been accustomed and used.' This meant all civil and criminal cases brought by those too poor to sue at common law and to try all cases of murder, felony, piracy, wrecking and such crimes likely to disturb the peace, as well as misgovernment, 'rumour-mongering' and adultery. Its duty was to administer the law cheaply and rapidly, dealing with some twenty cases a day. The oppressed and the poor flocked to it.

However, after the civil war, the politicians in Westminster did not want bits of the country ruling themselves. The Council was abolished in 1689. Now, if a Herefordian wanted justice, he would have to go to London instead of Ludlow.

Ludlow Castle, where Edward IV set up his Council of the Marches. (LC-DIG-ppmsc-08629)

AD 1609

OLD MEG GOODWIN

'THE COURTS OF kings for stately measures, the city for light heels and nimble footing, the country for shuffling dances, Western men for gambols, Middlesex men for tricks above ground, Essex men for the Hay, Lancashire for hornpipes, Worcestershire for bagpipes but Herefordshire for a Morris dance puts down not only all Kent but very near (if one had line enough to measure it) three quarters of Christendom.'

Such was the claim made in a pamphlet printed in London in 1609 called 'Old Meg of Herefordshire for a Maid Marian and Hereford town for a Morris dance', commemorating an extraordinary event in May of that year when twelve dancers, whose combined ages were over 1,000 years, performed in front of James I (although there is no official record of this King ever coming to Hereford) and other dignitaries at Hereford racecourse.

The names and ages of the participants are given. There were four 'whifflers', men whose infirmities precluded them from joining in and who were there to keep order: Thomas Price of Clodock (105 years old); Thomas Andres of Weston Beggard (108); William Edwards of Bodenham (108); and John Sanders of Walford (102).

The eleven male dancers were: James Tomkins of Llangarron (106); John

Will Kempe, the Shakespearian actor, dancing the Morris.

Willis of Dormington (97); Dick Phillips of Middleton (102); William Waiton of Marden (102); William Mosse, who had 'no moss at his heels' (106); Thomas Winney of Holmer (100); John Lace of Madley (97); John Carlesse of Holme Lacy (96); William Maio of Eggleton (97); John Hunt, 'the Hobby-Horse' (97); and John Mando, the Robin Hood, of Cradley (100).

But the only female dancer, who played the part of Maid Marian, put the rest in the shade. She was old Meg Goodwin, the famous wench of Eardisland, who was 120 years old and described herself as 'threescore years a maid and twenty years otherwise'.

James I, who watched Old Meg and her Morris men dance. (LC-USZ62-104640)

Their dress is described thus:

The musicians and the twelve dancers had long coats of the old fashion, high sleeves gathered at the elbows and hanging sleeves behind, the stuff, red buffin striped with white girdles with white stockings, white and red roses to their shoes; six had a white Jew's cap with a jewel and a long red feather, the others a scarlet Jew's cap with a jewel and a white feather; so the hobby horse and so the Maid Marian was attired in colours; the whifflers with long staves, white and red.

The event was meant to impress upon the King the remarkable longevity of Herefordshire people, attributed to the fine air. Lest anyone thought it was an unusual occurrence, the pamphlet assured its readers that it is easy to find 400 persons more within three years over or under 100 years of age.

The event seems to have passed off well, the only small mishap being that one of the dancers fell down and could not get up again. Of course, in an era before birth certificates, it would be difficult to ascertain the truth of their ages but they must have looked sufficiently ancient for people to believe the veracity of the claim.

It is good to know that there are still two Morris sides in Herefordshire carrying on this fine tradition: the Leominster Morris and the Silurian Border Morris, both dancing the variant known as Welsh Border Morris and both convinced they are the only side that is doing it properly.

There is also much contention over the origins of Morris dancing. Some think it is derived from 'Moorish dancing' and came from Spain in the late fifteenth century, at first as a courtly dance, only later being taken up by the people. Others (more mystic) believe it is the remnant of old fertility rites and the name derived from 'Mary's men' – hence Robin Hood and his 'merry' men and Maid Marian.

Certainly, like all pastimes of the poor, it was often regarded with deep suspicion by the authorities. On 2 December 1620, one William Edwards (a relation of the dancer who performed in front of the King?) was excommunicated for dancing the Morris at Wellington on the Sabbath day before evening prayer.

AD 1643

THE SIEGE OF BRAMPTON BRYAN

THE CAUSES OF the civil war were so complex that they are still giving rise to heated debate today. In short, Charles I thought he had a Divine Right to rule and therefore God was on his side, while the Parliamentarians thought he was making a complete hash of it and therefore God was on their side.

Most of the Herefordshire gentry, and therefore the people, sided with the King. There was, however, one who followed Parliament: Sir Robert Harley of Brampton Bryan, a staunch Puritan.

As war became inevitable, Parliamentary business kept Sir Robert in London, leaving his wife and three young children at Brampton Bryan Castle. Lady Brilliana was born at Brill near Rotterdam, where her father, Lord Conway, had been supporting the Dutch against Catholic Spain. Later Sir Robert entered Lord Conway's service and, although twenty years his junior, Brilliana found his Puritan views conducive and they had been married in 1623.

As war broke out Brilliana was desperate to travel to the safety of London, but her husband assured her that she was as safe in Herefordshire as anywhere. He was wrong. At the end of July 1643, a force of about 600 men set out from Hereford under the command of the Royalist Governor, Sir William Vavasour,

to remove this last outpost of Roundheads from the county.

Up against these soldiers Brilliana had about 100 employees, but these were mostly farm workers and servants (plus one old soldier from the Thirty Years War called Hakluit who her friends in Gloucester had managed to send her). To avoid bloodshed, Vavasour called on Lady Brilliana to surrender, being lifted up the castle walls in a basket. Her response was defiant. 'My dear husband has entrusted me with his house but according to his pleasure, therefore I cannot dispose of his house but according to his pleasure.'

The defenders were forced to watch as all the houses in the village were burnt down and their property and livestock plundered. Lady Brilliana, with her strong religious views, seems to have found some conditions of the siege particularly irksome. She complained in letters to her son, who was fighting with Cromwell, of the foul language that could be heard from the besiegers between bombardments, the fact that they placed their artillery in the churchyard and, possibly worst of all, that they had the temerity to continue fighting even on the Sabbath.

But, elsewhere in the country, things were not going the Royalists' way. Vavasour received news that the siege of Gloucester

Brampton Bryan Castle from the churchyard. (David Phelps)

was going badly, and decided to go and help, leaving his deputy, Harry Lingen, in charge.

Lingen continued the siege with increased vigour, using poisoned bullets and poisoning the stream that provided the castle with water. He was therefore responsible for the only two fatalities on the Roundhead side: Lady Brilliana's cook was hit by a poisoned bullet and died in great torment, and a poor, aged and blind man was killed by Lingen in the village street, for no apparent reason. However, the Royalist forces fared worse, being literally decimated: about sixty of their number were killed during the six weeks of the siege.

Then Lingen heard that the siege of Gloucester had been unsuccessful and was forced to go to the King's assistance. A group of labourers had held off an army six times their number. However, Lady Brilliana, who had not been in good health for some years, had been further weakened by the stress and privations of the siege. She died of pneumonia at the end of October.

Command of the castle now passed to the family doctor, Nathaniel Wright, and a second siege began in the spring of 1644. This time heavy cannon were brought against them and they could only hold out for three weeks before being forced to surrender. The castle was reduced, damaged so that it could not pose any further threat, as was Wigmore Castle, another of Harley's possessions. The prisoners, including Lady Brilliana's three young children, were taken to Shrewsbury, but were later released without harm. For his services Harry Lingen was knighted by the King the following year.

LETTERS OF BRILLIANA HARLEY

Like many of her class and period, Lady Brilliana was a constant letter writer. Even during the siege she managed to smuggle some out to her husband and eldest son. After her death the letters were forgotten in the family archives but were re-discovered and published in the middle of the nineteenth century. These excerpts give some idea of her misery:

At Ludlow they set up a Maypole and a thing like a head upon it, and so they did at Croft, and gathered a great many about it and shot at it in derision of Roundheads. At Ludlow they abused Mr Bauge's son very much, and are so insolent that they durst not leave the houses to come to the feast (church service). I acknowledge I do not think myself safe where I am. I lose the comfort of your father's company and am in but little safety but that my trust is in God and what is done in your father's estate pleases me not, so that I wish myself, with all my heart, in London ... but if your father think it best for me to be in the country, I am every way pleased with what he think best. I have sent by the carrier, in a box, three shirts, there is another but it is not quite made. I will, and it please God, send you another the next week and some handkerchiefs.... I pray God bless you and keep you from sin, and from all other evils, and give you a joyful meeting with
Your affectionate mother,
BRILLIANA HARLEY
June 4 1642

My dear Ned, I cannot but venture these lines, but whether you are in London or no, I know not. Now, my dear Ned, the gentlemen of this county have affected their desires in bringing an army against me. What spoils have been done, the bearer will tell you. Sir William Vavasour has left Mr Lingen with the soldiers. The Lord in mercy preserve me, that I fall not into their hands. My dear Ned, I believe you wish yourself with me; and I long to hear of you, who is my great comfort in this life. The Lord in mercy bless you and give me the comfort of seeing you and your brother.
Your most affectionate mother,
BRILLIANA HARLEY
August 25, 1643

I have taken a great cold, which has made me very ill these two to three days, but I hope the Lord will be merciful to me, in giving me my health for it is an ill time to be sick in.

My dear Ned I prey God bless you and give me the comfort of seeing you for you are the comfort of,
Your most affectionate mother,
BRILLIANA HARLEY
October 9, 1643

Lady Brilliana.

CLUBMEN

The trouble with civil war is that it is very difficult to keep out of it. The vicar of Tarrington, John Pralph, a man over eighty years old, was coming back from Hereford when he ran into some Parliamentary troopers, just come from making a nuisance of themselves in Ledbury, near the holy well at Stoke Edith. 'Who are you for?' one of the troopers cried. 'For God and the King,' Pralph replied, whereupon the trooper immediately shot him through the head.

But there were some who were determined to be neutral, mostly small farmers who were sick of the plundering that both sides brought down upon them. These 'clubmen', driven to distraction, themselves took up arms to maintain their independence.

On 18 March 1644 a mob of such men from Radnorshire and Herefordshire appeared outside the walls of Hereford demanding redress for the depredations heaped upon them, especially by the Irish garrison of Canon Frome. Governor Massey, the Parliamentary commander of Gloucester, arrived and urged them to join his cause as there was no room for a third party in England. Although his soldiers had only, so far, plundered the gentry, they refused him. Eventually Scudamore, the new governor, agreed to look at their demands and they dispersed. In Ledbury Prince Rupert was not so conciliatory: he hanged three of their leaders without trial.

NELL GWYN

WE KNOW FOR certain that Nell Gwyn was born on 2 February 1650 (the Feast of the Purification of the Virgin) at six o'clock in the morning, because, in later life, she had a horoscope made for that date and time. We are less certain of where she was born, although her grandson, who was Bishop of Hereford for forty years, never refuted the fact that she was born in Pipe Lane, just beside the walls of the Bishop's Palace.

Her father was of Welsh descent and a captain in the King's army during the civil war with a house in Hereford but, when records first speak of her, she was living at her mother's bawdy house near Drury Lane in London, though she always swore that she was never involved in the business of the house, other than as a domestic servant. Despite this, her enemies always believed that she had been a child prostitute.

With the restoration of Charles II, theatres were allowed to re-open, with the added excitement that women were now permitted to play female roles. Nell's mother knew 'Orange Moll', Mary Meggs, a former prostitute who had obtained the franchise for selling oranges to the audiences of the Theatre Royal, Drury Lane, and managed to get Nell a job. Orange selling was not a euphemism but a specific trade, keeping the audience amused before the performance as well as sometimes acting as a pander between the actresses and the young men who frequented the theatre. Oranges had only been recently introduced into the country and sold at the high price of sixpence; being able to sell them and keep a boisterous crowd entertained needed a sharp wit, something at which Nell excelled.

She made such a success of it that the management invited her, at the tender age of fourteen, to train as an actress. Plays at this period were given very short runs, the regular theatre-going public always demanding something new, so it is a tribute to Nell's memory (she seems to have been illiterate, always signing her name with a rather shaky E.G.) that she was able to master this trade. Soon, with her wit and charm, she was the most famous comic actress in London.

Naturally she attracted the attention of the King, an avid theatre-lover. Initially she demanded the shockingly high price of £500 a year for her services. Instead the Duke of Buckingham, Charles' own go-between, looked elsewhere: an actress in another company called Moll Davies. But, on the afternoon before Moll's first assignation, Nell took tea with her and managed to slip a laxative into the cake. Negotiations re-opened.

*Theatre Royal,
Drury Lane.*

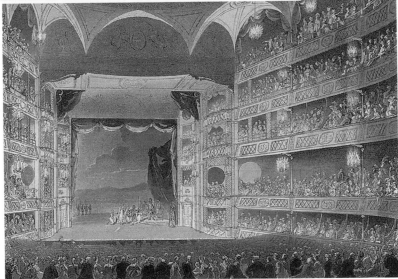

Inside the theatre.

The story goes that the King invited Nell, together with his brother James, Duke of York, to dine at an inn. However, when it came to pay neither Charles nor the Duke had any money: Nell had to pay, which she did with good grace, remarking, "Od's fish [a common expression of the King], but this is the poorest company I ever was in!'

Charles sent Lord Buckhurst, her current protector, on a pointless diplomatic mission and soon the court gossip was that the King had a new mistress, a position she held, though not without rivals, for the rest of Charles' life.

Although she did not amass the riches and titles that made other mistresses unpopular, she still did well out of the arrangement, Charles giving her a mansion on Pall Mall. This is still the only building on the south side of that road that is not owned by the Crown. She was also given a country house near Windsor, to be near the King when he was in residence there. It was here, annoyed by court laughter that her son by Charles had not been officially recognised, that she is supposed to have dangled the boy out of an upstairs window until the King gave him a title.

It was her wit that kept her in favour with both the King and the people. Once she came out of her house to find her coachman fighting with a bystander. Finding that it was because the man had called her a whore, she said, 'I am a whore. Find something else to fight about.'

An engraving of Nell from Beauties of the Court of Charles II, *showing a little of what Charles saw in her...*

Charles II. (LC-USZ62-38492)

Her lasting memorial is the Chelsea Hospital. Modern historians doubt her involvement, but records show she was present during discussions on suitable care for discharged soldiers. She would have recalled the Coningsby Hospital in Hereford, which performed the same purpose, as well as the dire end her father came to, dying in a debtors' prison.

She survived Charles by only three years, dying in 1687, at the age of thirty-seven. Although in debt, she left a bequest to the prisoners in Newgate. At her memorial service the Archbishop of Canterbury preached, taking as his sermon a text from Luke 15:7: 'I say unto you that likewise joy shall be in heaven over one sinner that repenteth, more than over ninety and nine just persons, which need no repentance.'

THESPIANS IN HEREFORD

Perhaps it was Nell Gwyn's example but Hereford produced many of the most famous actors on the eighteenth-century stage.

The most famous of these was David Garrick, born in a house on Widemarsh Street, though it was only fortuitous that he was born there, his father being in the army. He spent most of his childhood in Lichfield, where he was a pupil in Samuel Johnson's school. Johnson said of Garrick, 'his profession made him rich and he made his profession respectable.'

Roger Kemble came from an old established Herefordshire family. He was born in Church Street, Hereford, but, like many young people, had to leave the city to make his fame and fortune. He took to the stage, eventually joining the company of John Ward in Birmingham. He had the good sense to marry Ward's daughter and was thus able to set up his own travelling players. The couple had twelve children, of which five became noted actors.

Although often on the road, the Kembles had a house in St Peters Street, Hereford, but this burnt down in 1799, killing Roger's brother and a servant girl. The house was re-built but for many generations it was known locally as the Burnt House. The most famous of their children was Sarah, who became the foremost tragic actress of the day, especially famous for her Lady Macbeth. She married an actor called Siddons, and it is as Sarah Siddons that she was best known – although the marriage was not a happy one. Acting fashions change and her style might seem a little over-histrionic to our taste but, at the time, she could reduce a whole audience to tears.

Proud of its heritage, Hereford once had two theatres, the Kemble in Broad Street and the Garrick in Widemarsh Street. They are no more, the Kemble being replaced by one of the most hideous office blocks to be built in the 1960s and the Garrick replaced by a multi-storey car park.

Hereford man David Garrick as Richard III. (LC-DIG-pga-01034)

AD 1679

ST JOHN KEMBLE

O F ALL THE villains that have crawled across the pages of English history, none has cast a darker shadow than that of Titus Oates. He was a disgraced naval chaplain, only saved from hanging by his clerical status. In the feverish political world of Restoration London he saw his chance to make his fame and fortune. He went to the authorities with a completely fabricated tale of a plot to assassinate the King and replace him with his Catholic brother James. For a while his story was believed, until inconsistencies and obvious lies were discovered – but by then fifteen innocent men had gone to their deaths and his evil had spread as far as Herefordshire.

John Kemble was born at St Weonards in 1599, of a well-known Catholic family. John trained as a priest in France and returned to Herefordshire in 1625 to minister to his secret flock. Being a Catholic priest was no means as dangerous as it had been in Elizabeth's time but discretion was still needed. John spent most of his time at Pembridge Court near Welsh Newton, the home of his brother.

Somehow the name of this inoffensive priest was mentioned in connection with the plot to kill the King and he was arrested at his home by Captain John Scudamore of Kentchurch Court, whose own wife and children were regular members of Father Kemble's congregation. Despite his eighty years he was forced to make the difficult journey to London to answer for his crimes, walking under armed guard. At his trial he was found not guilty of any assassination plot but guilty of the treasonous act of being a Catholic priest, for which the only sentence was to be hanged, drawn and quartered.

To act as an example the sentence was to be carried out back in Hereford, so Kemble was made to make the arduous return trip, still on foot. Despite the 300-mile round trip, the demands of the trial and of being kept in a foul-smelling prison, he probably took no joy in reaching the end of his journey. The place of execution was to be Widemarsh Common. Before the terrible sentence was due to be carried out Father Kemble asked to be allowed to pray, a request which, in deference to his age, was granted him. He was also allowed one last drink and a pipe of tobacco, the under-sheriff, Mr Digby, joining him. Kemble finished his pipe first but graciously allowed Digby to finish his own smoke before they continued the affairs of the day. For many years after in Herefordshire a 'Kemble pipe' was the last smoke among friends before you started a journey.

John Kemble's grave, Welsh Newton.
(David Phelps)

St Francis Xavier's church, Broad Street, Hereford,
home to one of John Kemble's hands. (David Phelps)

Because of the dignity Father Kemble had shown he was allowed to strangle on the gallows before being cut down and disembowelled. The normal practice was for traitors to be still conscious when this was done. Then his body was cut up and the head and limbs distributed around the country as a warning to any others who might have traitorous intent. One of his hands can still be seen at St Francis Xavier's church in Broad Street, Hereford.

What was left of his body his brother was permitted to take back to Welsh Newton. Then came a strange twist to this bloody tale: soon various miracles were reported. John Scudamore's own daughter was cured of throat cancer by prayer to Father Kemble and Scudamore's wife had her hearing restored after praying at his grave. Kemble was eventually canonized in 1970 and his saint's day is 22 August.

CRUEL AND USUAL PUNISHMENTS

One of the top tourist attractions of Leominster Priory is a ducking stool, a wooden chair on a long beam on which the victim would be strapped and dunked in the river. This might seem rather quaint but it was actually a form of water-boarding and the sudden shock of being immersed in a cold river could prove fatal. Prior to the ducking the victim would be wheeled around town for public humiliation. It was a punishment reserved for nagging women and brewers and bakers who provided weak or short measure, with the magistrates stipulating the number of immersions.

The last person in England to be so treated was Jenny Pipes, 'a notorious scold' of Leominster in 1809, although Sarah Leake was sentenced to this punishment in 1817, also in Leominster. However, in Sarah's case the water level was found to be too low, so she was just paraded around the town instead.

We have all seen film representations of people being put in the pillory and being pelted with rotten fruit and vegetables but, if you had enemies in the crowd, they might decide to throw animal or human excrement instead, or even stones – in which case the punishment could prove fatal. Although the punishment only lasted a few hours, it still involved a stress position and was extremely uncomfortable, even on the rare occasions where the crowd was on the victim's side and threw nothing.

Being put in the stocks, a pillory just for the feet, does not sound too bad in comparison. However, this punishment could last for several days, with no toilet breaks and at the mercy of the weather: death could easily result from hypothermia or heat exhaustion. A person in the stocks was also in a very vulnerable position, and there were no rules against your enemies urinating or defecating on you while you were there. An extant stocks can be found in the village of Fownhope.

Such were the penalties for minor offences, but if you stole or killed someone then the penalty was death. For the

Ducking stool, Leominster Priory. (David Phelps)

The stool in operation. (Pearson Scott Foresman)

common people this was carried out by hanging: you would be suspended by the neck until your body weight strangled you, a process that could take from ten to twenty minutes. In was only in 1850 that a more merciful standard, the drop method, was introduced, with a drop of 4-6ft that should break the neck (although even this could go wrong and result in strangulation, as happened to the Nazi war criminal Ribbentrop). In 1872 the hangman James Berry developed a chart determining the correct drop depending on height and weight so that the victim would neither strangle nor be decapitated.

Nobles could be executed by the more merciful method of beheading, although modern science estimates that the brain can remain conscious for several seconds after the head is removed. It also demanded a skilled headsman, so it was a good idea to give him a few gold coins before the execution. The unfortunate record for having the most incompetent headsman is held by Margaret, Countess of Salisbury, whose execution in 1541 took ten strokes.

AD 1645

The Siege of Hereford

DURING THE LONG period of peace the people of Hereford had once again let their city walls get into a terrible state. So, in the first years of the war, the city was captured twice by the Parliamentarians with little opposition. Each time they made the wealthier citizens pay protection money to prevent looting and then retreated when threatened with the approach of Royalist armies.

Then, early in 1645, a new governor was appointed: Barnabas Scudamore. He set about repairing the walls and clearing the city ditch of rubbish and it was just as well he did so for, in July, news came that a Scottish army, 12,000 strong, fresh from their victory at Marston Moor and led by the Earl of Leven, was heading for the city.

The Scots were delayed by the poor Herefordshire roads which Leven described as the worst he had ever encountered. But, after destroying the Royalist garrison of Canon Frome, on Wednesday 30 July they arrived outside the gates of Hereford.

Scudamore had a force of 1,500 soldiers plus about 4,500 civilians. He greeted the Scots with a charge of cavalry over the Wye Bridge and an effective burst of musketry that caused several casualties and made the Scots more cautious.

Following the etiquette of war, Leven wrote to Scudamore, asking for his surrender. A city that accepts terms would not face the rape and pillage that would occur if it was taken by assault. Scudamore rejected the approach, saying he could only surrender on the orders of the King, and the Scots started to dig in. They built earthworks in the flat land of Bartonsham, to the east of the city, and strengthened the Row Ditch, a medieval defence-work in the Bishop's Meadow. Here they employed their nine siege guns to fire at the city, though their efforts were disrupted by occasional sallies from the city to attack their positions. One woman was hanged in High Town for letting the Scots know of the time of such a sally in return for money to feed her children.

The Scots concentrated their fire on the Wye Gate on the south side of the river so that it had to be abandoned, the defenders tearing down an arch of Wye Bridge and erecting a strong barricade at the bottom of Bridge Street. The Royalists also destroyed old St Martin's church to prevent it being used as an observation post.

The siege was a problem not only for the people in Hereford but for everyone in the county, as the Scots plundered outlying places for whatever they could find. The loot was taken back to their camps at Aconbury and Dinedor. Several hoards of coins dating from this period have been

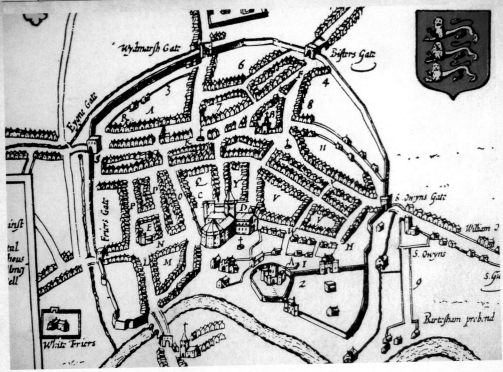

Map of sixteenth-century Hereford by John Speed.

Wye Bridge. The Scots were greeted with a charge of cavalry over the Wye Bridge and an effective burst of musketry that caused several casualties. (LC-DIG-ppmsc-08436)

found in the south of the county where people had tried to hide them. A raiding party was greeted in a friendly manner at Treago Castle near St Weonards: they were so surprised that they rode off without taking anything.

Elsewhere, the Scots tried mining underneath Friar's Gate but a little drummer boy, hearing vibrations from his drum and suspecting the cause, placed a pea on the instrument. When he saw the pea jump about he was certain. He raised the alarm, and the city ditch was diverted into the mine: the miners drowned. Fireballs made of cats, dogs and old horses with lighted torches tied to their tails were sent against the Scots' wooden defences in the night. On one occasion a bull, covered in pitch and a fire at its tail, was even sent against them.

Small boys were sent out at night, under covering fire, to set fire to the Scots' emplacements outside St Owen's Gate. At the end of August, heavy rain set in which lowered the morale of both sides. The Scots were also running low on ammunition but, to show they were not down-hearted, the townspeople organised a fox hunt on the walls.

When Leven's ammunition arrived he made a determined attack on Byster's Gate but was driven off. Then the Scots received news that the King, with a large force, was approaching and they were forced to raise the siege and retreat towards Newent. They lost about 1,200 men; ploughmen right up to the nineteenth century were turning over bones in the fields where they encamped. The Royalist dead amounted to twenty-one.

The King himself entered the city on 4 September. The church's bells, which had been silent during the siege, now rang out once again. Scudamore was knighted and Jane Merricke was also presented to the King. She had been in charge of a group of women repairing the defences at St Owen's Gate and had been badly injured.

Cromwell at Marston Moor: his army headed for Hereford.

The King showed his gratitude by augmenting the city's coat of arms. The three white lions were the differenced arms of Richard I, who had granted the city its first charter. Now the King awarded a new border of blue, with ten white saltire crosses for the ten Scottish regiments Hereford had repulsed. He also awarded the motto *Invictae Fidelitatis Praemium* (the reward for faithfulness unconquered) and, very rare in civic heraldry, the lion crest and, even rarer, a gold-barred peer's helm. The City of London is the only other municipal authority that has this honour.

High Town. A woman was hanged here for warning the Scots of an attack. (LC-DIG-ppmsc-08440)

A NEW TRICK TO TAKE TOWNS

It is always a good idea to be magnanimous in victory. That is a lesson the Royalists of Hereford had not learnt. Sir John Bridges, the owner of Wilton Castle near Ross, was determined to remain neutral. This displeased Scudamore and Lingen, who went to Wilton one Sunday when the household was at church and burned the castle down. Bridges, taking refuge in Gloucester, was determined on revenge. He had discussions with Colonel Morgan and Colonel John Birch, a Lancashire man who had lost his Bristol business because of the war and had successfully turned to soldiering. Using intelligence from disaffected Royalists, they determined a plan of taking Hereford.

By now it was December and the weather was freezing, with deep snow on the ground. Birch had a force of some 1,800 horse and foot. Birch went to Canon Frome and, from the garrison there, made up of tough men from the Forest of Dean, he chose six who could easily be disguised as simple countrymen. Others of his force seized the bridges of the Lugg, Lugwardine and Mordiford, so no word could come to Hereford. Then they marched to Aylestone Hill. Under cover of night a forward party was sent to the ruined Priory of St Guthlac at the bottom of the hill.

The Hereford garrison appears to have become very lax. Only the day before, Scudamore had found the guard at Byster's Gate too drunk to give the password. That night, because of either treachery or stupidity, it consisted of just four men, desperately trying to keep warm in below-zero conditions.

Dawn broke and at last the attackers heard reveille being beaten in the town. One of their muskets was discharged accidentally but, mysteriously, this did not alert the defenders. The gates were opened at eight o'clock. The disguised men went forward with bundles of bread and cheese and engaged the guards in conversation so that they did not see the force rushing out of the priory until it was too late. The guards were cut down by the spades and pickaxes carried by the 'workmen'.

The capture of the town took only half an hour and Birch lost only ten men. Only about fifty Royalists, including Scudamore and Lingen, escaped over the frozen river near the Bishop's Palace. Some of the citizens who tried to fight back were killed but most quickly surrendered. Because they had taken the city by assault, the soldiers set to plundering. In the next month Hereford fell into a terrible state, with dung left uncollected and many filthy beggars on the street. Some 800 Royalists were captured; sixteen notables, including the bishop, were sent to London and imprisoned. Dean Croft, incensed, preached in the cathedral against the troops' sacrilegious ways. Some musketeers were all for shooting him but Birch prevented them.

Scudamore went to Royalist Ludlow, where he was imprisoned until he could explain the loss of the city. Lingen and some other local cavaliers escaped to Goodrich. There they remained, despite some half-hearted attempts by Birch to extract them. Hearing that Birch and many of his men had been called to the Cotswolds, Lingen and thirty of his men attacked St Martin's Gate in broad daylight, killed the guards and entered the city. However, the population seems to have lost all heart for the fight and would not join him, and he was forced to return to Goodrich.

Birch, on his return, was determined to rid the county of this last nest of vipers, which he proceeded to do through cannon fire – including the largest mortar then existing, 'Roaring Meg', constructed at the nearby Old Forge. Described by the

cavaliers as 'no more than a toss-pot', it was still capable of firing a shot of 13lbs and soon brought down the Ladies' Tower and forced Lingen to surrender. The garrison was allowed to leave with banners flying and to a lively dance tune called *Sir Harry Lingen's Fancy*. He was kept under open arrest in Hereford on condition he did not wear his sword, a condition he soon broke. However, he was too popular in the city for Birch to act against him.

Scudamore, although cleared of a charge of incompetence over the loss of the city, never found favour again. He died in poverty in 1656. John Birch, along with Sir Robert Harley, fell out with Cromwell over the execution of Charles I. He was closely involved in negotiations to restore Charles II to the throne in 1660, for which he was richly rewarded, building up considerable estates in the county. After the Restoration

Charles I, who visited the city after the siege. (With kind permission of the Thomas Fisher Rare Book Library, University of Toronto)

Goodrich Castle then and now. (David Phelps and LC-DIG-ppmsc-08409)

he seems to have been involved in some very dodgy business dealings. However, he died a rich man, as his grandiloquent memorial in Weobley will testify.

In 1661 Dean Croft was appointed Bishop of Hereford. As if to spite his old adversary, he remained bishop as long as John Birch lived, dying in the same year, 1691. Sir Harry Lingen also returned to respectability with the Restoration, becoming one of the MPs for Hereford. However, within the year he caught smallpox and died on his way home, his body carried back to Stoke Edith church.

ROARING MEG

With a barrel diameter of 15ft 5ins, Roaring Meg could fire a ball of 2cwt filled with gunpowder. John Birch was so pleased with it that he personally fired the last nineteen balls of the siege.

DESTRUCTION OF HEREFORD CASTLE

Hereford had one of the earliest castles in England, and also one of the largest. John Leland, visiting in 1539, thought it to be as large as Windsor. It was originally built just before or just after the Norman Conquest. It commanded a strategic spot over the River Wye near the original ford that gave the town its name, although historians are not sure if that ford was at the site of the Old Bridge or near the Victoria Bridge. Whichever it was, no one was going to get across the river at this point without the agreement of the

Roaring Meg. (David Phelps)

The cathedral from Castle Green.

owner of the castle – which, for most of its existence, was the King.

With the introduction of gunpowder into the business of killing people, castles were no longer as safe as they had been. In the Wars of the Roses no commander thought it was a good idea to hole up in a castle. Better to face the enemy on the field of battle. Inevitably then, Hereford Castle, by the time Leland visited it, had already fallen into ruin and – the King always needing money – had been sold off into private hands.

However, the civil war gave it another lease of life and it and the city walls were refurbished by both Royalist and Parliamentarian garrisons. At the end of the fighting the castle was bought by Colonel Birch, although he preferred to live at the Bishop's Palace.

The victorious Parliament was anxious to prevent these defensive structures being used against them again in any renewal of the fighting. Furthermore, maintaining garrisons was expensive. Hereford Castle was ordered to be demolished in 1655, although Col. Birch argued against it, given its important position between North and South Wales. Also, 'the counties and people there were not so well affected as he could wish.' The great tower of the castle was taken down in April 1660, just a month before Charles II returned to England. The city authorities were not slow in taking advantage of the situation, selling the stone off to the Dean and Chapter of the cathedral and using the rest to build a toll house at the east end of High Town. Gravel from the mound was used for road repairs, repairs which were done so comprehensively over the next forty years that the site of the castle mound is now lower than the Castle Green.

At the beginning of the eighteenth century the Duke of Chandos proposed turning the Castle Green into his own private pleasure garden. As is usual in the city, people only realised the asset they had when it was in danger of being lost. We have Lord James Beauclerk, Bishop of Hereford and grandson of Nell Gwyn, to thank for establishing public walks there and, in 1752, the Society of Templars was set up to ensure the continuation of the Castle Green as a place of public enjoyment, something the Friends of the Castle Green maintain to this day.

THE GOODERE MURDER

SIR EDWARD GOODERE Bt was MP for Herefordshire from 1722 to 1727, after which he retired to his estate at Burhope near Wellington with a baronetcy given to him by the sleazy Prime Minister Sir Robert Walpole for services rendered.

He had a daughter and three sons. His daughter, Eleanor, married well, to John Foote, MP for Tiverton in Devon. His eldest son was groomed for succession; the second son, John, went into the merchant navy and his youngest son, Samuel, entered the Royal Navy.

Then disaster struck. Sir Edward's eldest son was killed in a duel in Ireland and John had to be recalled to take over the role. His father considered him more fit to be a bosun than a baronet and the two quarrelled bitterly. Misfortune also befell Samuel, who was court-martialled for 'having been very much wanting in the performance of his duty' in a naval action. He was found guilty and dismissed from his ship. He returned to Burhope and took his father's side in the continual rows that blighted the house.

John certainly seems to have been a brute. He mistreated his wife, driving her into the arms of another local squire, Sir Robert Jason. John took the pair to court and was awarded £500 damages. This might be the reason why, instead of educating his son as a gentleman, he apprenticed him to a saddler, the boy subsequently dying. It did not improve John's temper that his father and brother took his wife's part.

Sir Edward died in 1739, leaving more money to Samuel than to John but still less than Samuel had been expecting. The new Sir John promptly made a new will, leaving his estate to Samuel Foote, the son of his sister. For the next two years the two brothers were not on speaking terms, although Samuel did manage to get a new appointment, as captain of HMS *Ruby*.

On Sunday, 18 June 1741 fate brought the *Ruby* to Bristol. Captain Goodere heard that his brother was due to dine that evening with his attorney, Mr Smith, and sent a note to him saying that he very much wanted to mend the quarrel and asking leave to dine with them.

The two brothers spent the evening smoking and drinking together quite amicably. Samuel left first and went to the White Hart, where six sailors were waiting. They had already aroused the suspicion of the landlady as they had drunk nothing but tea all evening. As Sir John walked back to his lodgings he was seized by the sailors and dragged, screaming, to the quayside, where he was put aboard a boat and rowed to the *Ruby*.

Windsor Castle, where a murderer's son had a grace-and-favour apartment. (LC-DIG-ppmsc-08597)

Sir John was making such a fuss that some of the sailors became concerned but their captain assured them that this was a madman who was going to be confined to a cabin for his own safety. In the cabin were waiting two accomplices, Mahoney and White. Mahoney at first attempted to strangle Sir John with a handkerchief but this proved ineffective, only producing cries of 'Murder! Murder!' from Sir John. Captain Goodere then produced a rope and, with White holding the baronet down, Mahoney completed the deed.

Meanwhile the attorney Smith had heard that a man resembling his guest had been kidnapped and rowed to the *Ruby*. He obtained a warrant and boarded the ship, where he found Sir John's body. Mahoney and White had fled, but Captain Goodere was in custody. Sir John's cries had alerted the cooper and his wife. They had fetched the first lieutenant, Lt Berry, who had taken command and arrested his captain. Mahoney and White were quickly arrested, together with 350 guineas they had taken from the body. Later Sir John's watch turned up. White had given it to a woman of his acquaintance for safe keeping. She hid it in her privy but, when she heard what the fuss was about, she panicked and brought it to the authorities.

They were brought to trial on 26 March. Samuel's defence was that his brother was insane and, in a fit of madness, had strangled himself. The jury did not believe it and the three men were sentenced to hang. This was carried out on 15 April, within sight of the *Ruby*. The bodies of Mahoney and White were given to the surgeons for dissection but Captain Goodere, being a gentleman, was, after a day's delay to prevent attempts at reviving him, brought back to Burhope where he was buried at dead of night, near his brother.

Of Samuel's two sons, one died in a lunatic asylum and the other, reduced to poverty, was given a grace-and-favour apartment in Windsor Castle where he became a noted eccentric, drawing huge crowds to watch his daily perambulations.

A FAMOUS GRANDSON

Edward Goodere's grandson, Samuel Foote, married an heiress, Mary Hicks. He seems to have been genetically a Goodere, for 'his peculiarities ranged from the harmless to the malevolent'. On inheriting the larger fortune of the Gooderes he deserted her, and she died in poverty.

Samuel squandered both fortunes and was forced to go on the stage, where he became a noted comic actor.

THE WYE TOUR

Tourism was invented in Herefordshire. From the end of the seventeenth century the sons of the nobility and gentry had been packed off to Europe to take part in the Grand Tour, at worst to sow their wild oats, at best to pick up a bit of culture – often literally, the country houses of the nation being packed with souvenirs collected on these travels. But, as the middle class became more affluent through the eighteenth century, they sought to emulate their betters and also travel for pleasure rather then just business.

Then William Gilpin published *Observations on the River Wye and several parts of South Wales etc. relative chiefly to Picturesque Beauty, made in the summer of 1770*. Despite its snappy title it became a bestseller, encouraging people to actually look at the landscape and countryside rather than getting through it as quickly

A satirical letter aimed at Samuel Foote, whose impressions of various public figures on the stage caused public outrage. (LC-USZ62-137505)

Samuel Foote.

Goodrich, one of the highlights of the tour.

The picturesque Wye at Symonds Yat. (David Phelps)

as possible to get to somewhere interesting. In particular people were told to look out for the Picturesque –'that peculiar kind of beauty which is agreeable in a picture.'

With the outbreak of the Revolutionary and Napoleonic Wars closing Europe to British travellers, more and more people came to Ross to take the tour, with as many as ten pleasure boats catering for their needs, equipped with drawing tables, canopies to prevent sunstroke and local men to steer and row; although hardier or poorer souls such as William Wordsworth preferred to walk along the river banks.

From Ross the boats would travel to Goodrich, considered the second most picturesque sight on the tour, then down to the iron works at New Weir, also considered picturesque, and so on to Symonds Yat, there being no rapids there at the time (these being a modern invention to please canoeists).

After spending the night in one of the inns of Monmouth, travellers would come to what was considered the highlight of the tour, Tintern Abbey, especially after Wordsworth penned his lines on the subject, and so on to Chepstow.

Inevitably the hordes of incomers caused some dismay among locals who had no way to profit from them. Tourists, as now, were mocked for their ignorance and arrogance, most notably in William Combe's *Adventures of Dr Syntax*, a book that many modern tourists could profitably read before embarking on their excursions.

The Wye Tour survived the Picturesque movement and remained popular until the middle of the nineteenth century, when seaside holidays became fashionable. Sadly, no pleasure boats make the journey today. If you want to see the glories of the Wye now you must take your life in your hands in a canoe.

AD 1786

THE COLLAPSE OF THE CATHEDRAL

EVERYONE WHO HAS a house to maintain knows that the price of keeping a roof over your head is eternal vigilance, although the Dean and Chapter of Hereford Cathedral had a harder job than most. Like all the twenty-six medieval cathedrals of England, Hereford is a mongrel of architectural styles. It was built between 1079 and 1530, as fashions changed and the cathedral authorities' finances waxed and waned. The seventeenth century was not kind to the fabric of the building. Not only had it been in the centre of several sieges but, when the Parliamentary army took over, it had no love or care for an institution that had an aura of Popery. They let the place decline. John Aubrey, the antiquarian, reports that, in the crypt below the Lady Chapel, which he described as 'the greatest charnel-house for bones, that ever I saw in England', there lived, in 1650, a poor old woman that 'to help out her fire, did use to mix the dead men's bones: this was thrift and poverty.' She also seems to have sold some of the bones to local ale-wives to put in their ale 'to make it intoxicating'.

At Restoration the neglect continued. The cathedral looked quite different to its current appearance, having a west tower as well as a central tower, the later with a spire built in the late fifteenth century.

Throughout the eighteenth century there were various alarms about the integrity of the building and attempts made to rectify it but, during the penitential season of Lent in 1786, serious cracks were appearing on the west tower, though services continued as normal.

On Easter Monday, 17 April, it finally collapsed, taking with it half the Norman nave. Bishop Beauclerk died soon after, possibly the second bishop, after Athelstan in 1055, to have his life cut short by shock at the damage to the cathedral. Much discussion went on as to the need to repair the tower or whether it did not look better with just a central tower. It would also make repair cheaper. This was decided upon and the renowned architect James Wyatt was appointed to oversee the work.

The historian A.T. Bannister describes the appointment of Wyatt as the second worst disaster that befell the cathedral since 1079. He was intent on removing as much of the original structure as he could and replacing it with 'Gothic' stylings of his own design and shortened the nave by one bay. During his surveys it was also discovered that the central tower had been weakened and the spire in danger of collapse, so this was removed. During the operation two masons, called Pember and Prosser, fell from the tower and were killed.

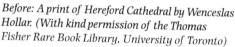

After: A print by James Wathen.

Before: A print of Hereford Cathedral by Wenceslas Hollar. (With kind permission of the Thomas Fisher Rare Book Library, University of Toronto)

The Wyatt west front was never popular, an unworthy termination of the massive Norman church. On the death of Queen Victoria it was decided to erect a memorial and the women of the diocese subscribed for a new west window. This inspired Dean Leigh to raise funds for a new western façade to the nave using a design of Oldrid Scott, son of the famous Gilbert Scott. Unfortunately, instead of using local sandstone, Scott chose red stone from Staffordshire and some of the sculpture has been described as insipid. So the cathedral never recovered from Easter Monday, 1786.

AD 1821

TOM SPRING

TOM WINTER WAS born at Rudgend near Fownhope in 1795. He was encouraged to take up boxing by his father, who made him a punch bag to help his training. But his father was imprisoned for debt and Tom was apprenticed to a butcher in Mordiford. He retained his interest in the sport and it was while he was fighting in a local bout that he caught the eye of Tom Cribb, the heavyweight champion of England.

Cribb persuaded Tom to go to London to try his luck and it was then he acquired his fighting name of Tom Spring in reference to his constant moving about the ring. He was the most athletic of early boxers, the Mohammed Ali of his day, with no strong punch but a stout defence and effective left hook. He perfected the so-called Harlequin step, standing just within reach of his opponent, avoiding the inevitable punch and then getting his own in when his opponent was unbalanced. He had nine professional fights in which he was defeated only once (by the Bristolian Ned Painter, although this was a re-match, Spring having previously defeated him). Unlike most professional prize fighters, he never suffered a serious injury.

In 1821 Tom Cribb retired and handed the heavyweight championship to Spring, who commenced a tour of the country offering to fight any man who cared to come forward. No one did until 1823, when another Bristol man, Bill Neate, took up the challenge. Psyching out your opponent is nothing new to the sport and Neate called Spring a 'lady's maid fighter'. The event was an anti-climax, Spring defeating Neate in thirty-seven minutes, over eight rounds.

In was then that Spring engaged in his most famous series of fights with the Irishman John Langan. Langan was the opposite in style to Spring, being slower and heavier. The first fight took place on Worcester Racecourse on 7 January 1824. An estimated 30,000 people turned up: such was the crush of the crowd that the grandstand collapsed, injuring many. The crowd was so dense that they had to be driven out of the ring by men with whips, and the bout had to be suspended on several occasions when fights broke out in the crowd which boiled over into the ring. It lasted two and a half hours – seventy-seven rounds. Spring's left hand was useless and his right caused him agony at each punch, but Langan was so battered that the crowd shouted for the match to be stopped, which eventually it was.

The re-match, at Chichester in June, still attracted a crowd of 15,000. Langan tried to make use of his wrestling skills to

A typical Georgian boxing ring.

weaken Spring, whose left hand had still not recovered and was said to resemble a steak pudding. Slowly, however, Spring gained the upper hand. By the seventeenth round Langan's face was unrecognisable, but still he fought on. In the end Spring resisted giving the brave fellow the *coup de grace*, but simply pushed him over with an open hand. The fight had lasted one hour and forty minutes, over seventy-six rounds.

But Spring's hands were now so injured that he decided to retire. He was now wealthy, so he got married and took ownership of the Booth Hall in Hereford. In 1828 he set up the Fair Play Club to improve prize-fighting's image, it generally being considered even worse than racing for corruption and betting scandals. Not that Tom Spring was above such things. He managed the Irish boxer Simon Byrne and, on at least one occasion, let Byrne fight knowing he was unfit and sure to lose.

Tom Spring and his opponent, Langan.

When Bryne fought the then heavyweight champion James Burke the fight lasted ninety-nine rounds, the longest in the history of the sport. This record held until 1893. In the last round Byrne was so groggy that Spring had to support him to the mark. Burke was not as merciful as Spring had been, and quickly knocked the unfortunate man out. Byrne never regained consciousness, and died three days later. This led to the tightening of boxing regulations.

In 1846 Spring moved to the Castle Tavern in Holborn, deserting his wife, who died in a workhouse. Spring did not long outlive her, dying in 1851 – allegedly of the curse of the publican's life, being too fond of his product. He is buried in West Norwood cemetery but his fans in Herefordshire subscribed to a memorial to him: a cider mill set in a field near his boyhood home.

CIDER, SHEEP AND BULLS

Herefordshire was once the most rural county in England. In 1911, 8 per cent of the county was covered by woodland, with another 5 per cent orchards.

Of course, everything on this earth is subject to change. Hops, once a familiar sight in the fields, are now little grown. Perhaps one of the sayings about their cultivation, 'Certain care, uncertain profit', can explain why this is so.

Cider has been drunk in these parts since Celtic times, indeed once forming a part of a labourer's wages until this was made unlawful by the Truck Acts at the beginning of the nineteenth century.

Specialist cider apples were known to the Saxons, but it was at the end of the seventeenth century that varieties still used today – Redstreak, Kingston Black and Gennet-Moyle etc. – appeared. In 1887 the son of the rector of Credenhill, too delicate to take up one of the professions, took the advice of his mother, to find 'something to do with eating or drinking, because they never go out of fashion.' He made his first two casks of cider and the firm of Bulmers was born.

Every county used to have its own variety of sheep most suited to local conditions, and Herefordshire's was the Ryeland, so called because it could live on the aftermath after the harvesting of a rye crop. It produced top-quality wool, known in the Middle Ages as 'Lemster ore', which was shipped to Bruges and Florence. Elizabeth I was presented with stockings made from Ryeland wool and was so pleased that she swore after to wear no other type of wool.

Hereford cattle, which make the county well known throughout the world, were developed by selective breeding at the beginning of the eighteenth century, designed for beef rather than the all-purpose use – most especially ploughing – that animals had previously been bred for. By the end of the Napoleonic wars Hereford cattle were fetching higher prices than any other breed, though it was only in the 1840s that the breed developed the white face and red coat that is now characteristic. While the bull is noted for his placid temper, heaven help you if you get between a Hereford cow and its calf.

AD 1861

DEMOLITION OF
THE OLD TOWN HALL

VISITORS TO NORTHERN European cities often marvel at the magnificent old town halls such places often contain. Built in stone or wood, in the sixteenth and seventeenth centuries, their intricate carvings are a symbol of civic pride. It can come as a shock to be told that Hereford once possessed one to equal, if not surpass, any to be seen on the Continent.

It was probably built in High Town during the last years of the sixteenth century and is therefore too early to have been built by John Abel, the noted builder of other market halls in the county, to whom it is often attributed, although this just shows the wealth of carpentry talent the county possessed.

It stood on twenty-seven wooden columns, arranged in three rows of nine, and was 84ft long and 34ft wide (although a lantern on top took its height to over 100ft). It was the largest building of its kind in England. Pevsner, in his *Buildings of England*, describes it as a sight to thrill any visitor from England or abroad, and 'the most fantastic black and white building imaginable'. There were three storeys, the first floor being used for the law courts, while the second floor had chambers for the guilds most important to the city, namely bakers, barbers, barber-surgeons (who performed simple surgery), braziers (brass workers), butchers, coopers, cordwainers (shoe makers), glovers, mercers (cloth merchants), tanners, tilers and weavers. As the importance of guilds decreased the space was used by the mayor and aldermen. The open space below the hall was used as a market.

By the end of the eighteenth century the pressure exerted by the building on its timber piers was causing alarm and the decision was taken to remove the upper storey in 1792. The building was also covered in fashionable plaster-work

Hereford old Town Hall in all its glory.

Hereford Town Hall after the removal of the upper storey.

given: that it would allow traffic to flow more freely (where have we heard that one before?); and that people's sensibilities were being affronted by the slaughter of cattle in the market place. So the market was moved further north in the city's continual attempt to move the source of its prosperity further from the centre.

Coloured paving in High Town shows where it stood and how extensive it was. The only pieces of the Town Hall still in existence are two quarter jacks, wooden figures that struck bells on the quarter hour, which are now in the museum. Some of the wood from the Town Hall was used to make a gavel to keep councillors in order – and also, it is hoped, to serve as a reminder that not all their decisions are the right ones.

to obscure its rustic look. But problems persisted and eventually the building was declared too unsafe for important people like the council to meet in it. Repairing it was going to cost money so, in 1861, the momentous decision was taken by the council to tear the whole building down, an act Pevsner describes as 'a memorable piece of municipal vandalism (and stupidity)'.

With it went the High Cross and the Toll House, as well as a row of other black and white houses, leaving only one, now known as the Old House. Apart from cost of repair, various other reasons were

The city eventually got a new Town Hall in 1904, although there have been recent rumours that consultants consider that this is now itself too expensive and out of date and should be sold off. Arguments have been made that the old hall should be re-built – its loss is still keenly felt in the town – on the grounds that doing so would incur a far smaller cost than building the new shopping mall planned for the site to which the market was moved, and that the project would awaken the city's once great carpentry skills. Opponents say it has gone – get over it.

RURAL STRIFE!

LIFE FOR THE Herefordshire peasant remained unchanged for 1,000 years, apart from the vagaries of war, pestilence and his master. All this changed in the eighteenth century. An unholy alliance of landowners, farmers and the Church of England realised that the land they owned was a valuable asset. They determined to get as much profit out of it as possible. Previously land was farmed in large open fields, which provided most villagers with a degree of self-sufficiency. An increasing and agriculturally unproductive urban population created a market for surplus food, and the rich were determined to cater for this by enclosing fields and rationalising holdings so that modern farming techniques could be employed. This could only be done by Act of Parliament but the meeting to formalise the plea to Parliament was often not publically advertised and held a long distance away to make sure only the right people attended. MPs, themselves landowners, were blind to such shady practices.

The compensation workers received for their loss was soon gone, and men who had once been able to support themselves became day labourers, being shouted at by farmers sitting on horses who, a few years before, had worked side by side with them.

Workers' cottages might look quaint but were often dilapidated. (Bustin Collection, Hereford Record Office)

Sydney Box and colleagues at the Three Shires Show, 1925.

To make matters even worse, repressive Game Laws, aimed at protecting the sport of the rich, could send a man to prison for three months for catching a rabbit to feed his family.

Herefordshire was considered a quiescent county. Only one person was convicted of taking part in the 'Captain Swing' riots of 1830, perhaps because the area had very few of the threshing machines that were the target of the disturbances. This unfortunate man, Henry Williams, aged twenty, was found guilty of writing a threatening letter to a farmer and was sentenced to fourteen years' transportation.

However, protest can take many forms. Landowners and farmers who were thought to have transgressed the unwritten laws governing how workers were to be treated could face other sanctions, including having their animals maimed, their crops stolen or burnt, their game poached, or their sheep and wood supplies taken. In 1811 Lady Rodney of Berrington Hall offered a reward of 100 guineas for the apprehension of the person who wrote an incendiary letter and left it inside a cannon near the hall, and another 100 for the person who shot and wounded her gamekeeper. Despite this being equivalent to winning the lottery, no one came forward. In rural areas, perpetrators of murder or of sexual offences were quickly apprehended, thanks to the help of the populace, but poachers and the like, in tight-knit communities, were difficult to catch.

In hard times farmers' tithes to the Church, a tenth of their crop, were especially resented. It was felt that if the farmers did not have to pay these they could raise wages. Equally, the large amounts being spent on renovation of churches throughout the century were unpopular: the money, the populace felt, would be better spent helping the poor. Many chose to answer adverts – which frequently appeared in local papers – offering jobs in Birmingham, or even further afield.

With the rise of Unionism in the 1870s, Thomas Strange and William Ward represented Herefordshire at the formation of the National Agricultural Labourers' Union. It was an uphill struggle, with men risking dismissal for joining, although the media, in the shape of the *Hereford Times* and *Hereford Journal*, supported their actions. At the turn of the century Sidney Box took up the fight. Two of the few establishment figures who supported him were the historian Canon Bannister and Alfred Watkins, the inventor of the concept of ley lines. But the economic depression of the post-war years reduced membership and life remained harsh. Many would agree with a placard seen at a riot in Ross in 1853 demanding 'A Large Loaf of Bread and Plenty of Everything.'

AD 1893

THE LONGTOWN HARRIERS

JANUARY 1893 WAS a cold one, with snow on the ground. These were bad times in the tiny village of Clodock, tucked against the Black Mountains, and there was little respite from the fight for survival.

A farmer's young child had died and was buried in the frozen earth of the churchyard and, as was the custom, this was seen as an opportunity for drinking at the nearby Cornewall Arms, a ramshackle, white-washed cottage near the churchyard. As the *Hereford Times* later reported, 'total abstinence from intoxicating liquors is not one of the cardinal virtues of the parish.'

The music was provided by William Prosser, a man of some thirty years of age, slim and about 5ft 4in tall, playing his melodeon; the popular drink of the evening was 'rum hot', mulled beer mixed with rum.

Despite his musical prowess, William was not popular in the village, being suspected of stealing other people's chickens (which could be a serious loss in this poor village). He saw that things were getting a bit boisterous for his liking and left for home around 9.30p.m, to shouts of derision. He made for his cottage about a mile away, where he lived alone since his parents had moved to a neighbouring parish. The drinking continued far longer

than the normal closing time, aided by the fact that the constable had been called away. Eventually it was down to half a dozen young men who, for a prank, took a side of bacon that was hanging by the chimney and threw it in the fire. Then they were shown the door.

But they had no wish to end the night's entertainment yet and had a snowball fight in the road outside. When this palled, they got to thinking about Prosser and how he had got away with the theft of their chickens. They went to a nearby hayloft where they found John Cross, a fifty-year-old mason from Leominster whom they suspected of being in league with Prosser. They dragged him outside and rolled him in the snow for a bit. Then they went to the house of Edwin Chappell, another friend of Prosser's. They broke into his house, picked him out of his bed and threw him into the icy River Monnow. Fortunately the river was shallow at this point, and Chappell was able to extricate himself.

By this time the young rowdies had crossed the footbridge and were heading for Hunthouse Cottage, where Prosser lived.

They started smashing his windows. Prosser, in a panic, dressed hurriedly and jumped out of his bedroom window, but was seen – and a chase began. William

Clodock churchyard. (David Phelps)

Cornewall Arms, Clodock, where the evening's events began. (David Phelps)

had only crossed one field when his hastily put-on trousers fell off and he was forced to run through the snow in bare feet and just a shirt and waistcoat. He ran to the cottage of a friend but could not gain entry before the pack was on him. In desperation, he fled to another friend's, who lived at Ashtree Cottages, opposite the churchyard, but, on dashing through the gate, his shirt and waistcoat got caught on the top of the gate and, despite his strenuous efforts, he could not free himself.

Inexplicably, he appears to have shaken off his pursuers at this point. However, his terrified cries attracted no attention, and he was forced to hide, half-naked, in the snow. He froze to death. His last sight was that of the churchyard where he would soon be buried.

His body, in a seated position, was found the next morning and the police called in. Their initial investigations were hampered by the reticence of the villagers, who were considered clannish even by Herefordshire village standards.

But eventually five men were indicted to stand trial for manslaughter at the Shire Hall in Hereford. They were: Leonard Miles (thirty-two), farmer; John Williams (twenty-one), farmer's son; William Davies (thirty-four), miller; Walter Griffiths (also known as Boucher), labourer; and Thomas Jones, also a labourer.

All five pleaded guilty and, because the judge accepted that they did not have murderous intent and because of their previously blameless characters, he gave them what he considered light sentences: Davies and Griffiths were sentenced to one year's penal servitude with hard labour, and the other three to four months', also with hard labour.

Market wits soon christened the men from the area 'the Longtown Harriers', although it was not a name you wanted to say aloud if anyone from Clodock walked into the pub. The *Hereford Times* epitaph on the incident, from the now near-forgotten writer Robert Martin, was, 'Faith, we never know what we'll be up to next.'

AD 1914-1918

THE HEREFORDSHIRE REGIMENT IN THE FIRST WORLD WAR

AT THE START of the First World War, the Herefordshire Regiment was a Territorial Force, but it was one of the first to volunteer for overseas service. It remained in a reserve capacity – but then some bright spark, Winston Churchill, suggested a diversionary attack against Turkey to relieve the pressure on the Western Front. This did not go too well, so another diversionary attack – this time to relieve the pressure at Gallipoli – was planned.

The Herefords landed at Suvla Bay on 9 August 1915, at 7.20 a.m., in support of the Gallipoli landing. Almost immediately they were ordered to the front line, to

Officers of the Herefordshire Regiment, September 1914. (Hereford Times)

support the right flank of the Sherwood Foresters. There were no maps of the position but Major Carless led B and C companies forward. They immediately came under sustained artillery fire. The terrain was rough ground, mostly covered with scrub. The last part of the journey was completed under hot rifle fire. Then the order came from Corps HQ for the battalion to return to their original position.

However, the following morning, they were ordered back to the Sherwood Foresters' position. Sir Ian Hamilton, the commander in chief, now ordered a suspension of operations, even though he was opposed by a relatively small Turkish force. Then followed a period of trench warfare which was made wearisome by the heat and the flies, while dysentery both

rapidly spread and became very serious; casualties rose to appalling numbers. Here, instead of Flanders' mud, there was bare rock in which, under fire, the Herefords had to dig defences.

By 7 December the Herefords were reduced to a strength of 130 men in the line. The Division commenced to withdraw on 11 December. They left from exactly the same bit of the beach on which they had landed just eighteen weeks before. Back on that bright and sunny morning in August, the battalion had been 750 men strong. On that dark December night they numbered 100, all weary, dirty and disillusioned.

The regiment went on to serve in Egypt, Palestine and France but, for many, those few weeks in 1915 typified the waste of the 'war to end wars'.

AD 1916

TRAGEDY AT THE THEATRE

IN THE FIRST World War, just as in present conflicts, the people back home wanted to do what they could for the heroes at the front. Many in Herefordshire had fathers, brothers, husbands or sweethearts involved in the conflict.

A group of Hereford women decided to organise a fund-raising concert at the Garrick Theatre in Widemarsh Street to provide treats to men of the Herefordshire Regiment then in Egypt. The concert was set for April 1916 and involved a large cast of over forty performers, most of them the young daughters of servicemen.

After an entertaining show of songs and short sketches given to a packed audience mostly made up of proud relations of the performers, the grand finale was a representation of a winter wonderland. Dressed in cotton wool costumes of Eskimos and ice maidens, and pulling the little ones on sledges, the little girls trooped on stage as confetti snow fell from above. They had a mock snowball fight and then started throwing the snowballs at the audience, to laughter and applause and the snowballs being returned by the more exuberant members. Many people thought of their loved ones sweltering in Egypt, where temperatures were sometimes 130 degrees Fahrenheit in the shade, and wished they could be there to see this.

Eventually the curtain dropped and the little girls, excited by their success, walked off. Suddenly, however, tragedy struck: one of the girls passed too close to an open flame, and gave a terrified shriek as her cotton-wool costume caught fire. As she panicked and tried to beat it out, the flames spread to the costumes of other

The Hereford Times *reports the tragedy.*
(Hereford Times)

The tragic victims.
(Hereford Times)

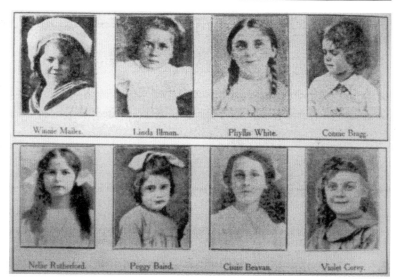

Winnie Mailes.   Linda Henan.   Phylls White.   Connie Bagg

Nellie Rutherford.   Peggy Baird.   Cissie Beavan.   Violet Corey.

performers. Supervising mothers and their helpers tried desperately to help, and were themselves burned. Somebody called out 'Fire!', creating more panic in the audience, some of whom tried to escape; others fought to get to the stage to find their daughters. Fleeing crowds alerted people in Widemarsh Street and beyond, and soon a great crowd had gathered, some of them parents anxious for news of their children. Rumours flew, but the truth was eventually ascertained: six children had died and another two had been rushed to hospital with terrible injuries.

At the inquest a pompous coroner had an argument with one of the fathers because a neighbour had tried to 'interfere with his office' by advising the fellow not to view the body of one of the girls because the sight was too horrible.

The shock felt in the city was tremendous. It was felt that a civic funeral should be arranged for the following Thursday, which was half-day closing. Flags were flown at half mast and shops and houses closed their shutters as a mark

of respect. Crowds lined the route of the procession. The parents of one of the victims decided that they wanted a private ceremony, so five small coffins were carried through the streets of Hereford to the cathedral, accompanied by the sound of muffled church bells. After the service the crowd followed the coffins to the cemetery at Westfaling Street, where they were buried with all due ceremony.

In the next few days the two badly injured girls both died, bringing the death toll to eight. One can barely imagine the feelings of the fathers on active service when they were told the news that their daughters had been killed back in the safe old city of Hereford.

An inquiry was opened into the tragedy, held at the Shirehall. Little damage had been caused to the theatre and no fault was found with the electrics. One girl gave evidence that 'a man lit a cigarette and threw down the match', but no evidence was found to corroborate this story and the verdict was returned of accidental death.

AD 1922

THE HAY POISONER

MAJOR HERBERT ROWSE Armstrong was a pillar of the establishment in Hay-on-Wye. He had practised as a solicitor in the town since 1906 and was a prominent freemason and staunch member of the Conservative Party. Although of humble origins, he had worked hard to achieve this position and now lived at the substantial property of Mayfield in Cusop Dingle with his wife and three children. In the First World War he had risen to the rank of major in the Royal Engineers Territorial Force, and afterwards referred to himself as Major Armstrong.

But his marriage was not a happy one. Mrs Armstrong seemed disappointed in her husband and often publically humiliated him. Local people had no doubts who wore the trousers in the marriage.

Then, in May 1919, Kitty Armstrong fell ill with gastric pains. These became so bad that she was admitted to a private mental asylum near Gloucester, where her condition improved. She was released in January 1921. However, when she returned home, her condition once again deteriorated. She died on 22 February, her husband solicitously attending on her until the last. Few came to her funeral.

Oswald Martin was Armstrong's rival in Hay. They had become involved in a complicated and prolonged dispute over an estate which, when settled, looked likely to cost Armstrong a substantial sum of money. In an effort to sort the problem out Armstrong invited Martin to tea at Mayfield but, in the event, the dispute was not discussed. Instead they talked of mundane affairs and Armstrong talked about his loneliness and Martin's luck to be happily married. During the tea Armstrong handed Martin a buttered scone with the words, 'Excuse my fingers!'

On returning home Martin fell violently ill. As luck would have it, Martin's father-in-law was John Davies, the local chemist. He was called and was struck by the similarities of the symptoms to arsenic

Major Armstrong.

Mayfield, the Armstrongs' home. (David Phelps)

poisoning. He recalled selling Armstrong a large quantity of arsenic, the major saying it was for his dandelions – although, being October, these plants were no longer a serious problem.

Then a box of chocolates was delivered anonymously to the Martins. This time Dorothy Martin, Oswald's brother's wife, fell ill after eating one. Davies contacted the Home Office. The chocolates were examined and found to contain arsenic and, at their base, a small needle hole through which it had been inserted. During the dead of night Mrs Armstrong's body was exhumed. It was found to contain huge amounts of arsenic.

The major was arrested at his Broad Street offices on 31 December 1921 and brought to trial in Hereford on 3 April 1922. He pleaded not guilty. Local gossip seemed to agree with him, pointing out that this was a copy of a previous case last year when another Hay solicitor, Harold Greenwood, had been acquitted of his wife's murder: only members of the Martin family had fallen ill, and they were closely connected to a man who would know all about the symptoms. Was Armstrong

being framed by a rival? However, others pointed to the death of William Davies, an estate agent in Hay, who had also been in dispute with Armstrong and had died unexpectedly in October 1921, just when the Martins started falling ill. Perhaps Kitty Armstrong was not the only victim?

Armstrong's defence was that his wife committed suicide: she had apparently often talked about it. But medical evidence was heard that, in her last days, Mrs Armstrong was completely paralysed. Major Armstrong still insisted that he only bought arsenic in order to control his dandelions, but could not explain why he had a pouch of the stuff in his pocket when he was arrested in December.

Although the evidence against him, though compelling, was only circumstantial, Armstrong was found guilty and sentenced to hang. All appeals failing, the sentence was carried out at Gloucester Gaol on 31 May 1922. Newspapers reported his last words as, 'I'm coming, Kitty!', although the hangman later said that they were, 'I am innocent'. He is still the only solicitor ever to be hanged for murder.

AD 1931

ALL HAIL KING ANTHONY!

WE HAVE ALL fantasised about what it would be like to be King or Queen, but most of us grow out of it. Anthony Hall never did; he was still proclaiming himself the rightful King of England up until the day he died.

He certainly had good connections, being the nephew of a High Sheriff of Herefordshire. He had been born in London in 1898 but moved to Herefordshire with his family a few years later. In the First World War he had served as an ambulance driver, seeing action at the Somme and being gassed at Ypres. After the war he joined the Shropshire police, rising to the rank of inspector. He left the police after being left a fortune by his father, and by 1931 he was living quietly at Little Dewchurch. Perhaps it was his experiences in the war, or perhaps he had listened to family stories, but, in that year, he launched his campaign to assume his proper place on the throne.

He claimed that he was a direct descendent of Thomas Hall, a man who he claimed was the bastard son of Henry VIII and Anne Boleyn. He further claimed that the real James I had been murdered as an infant and secretly replaced by 'Goggle-eyed Jimmy' Erskine, whose head was too big for his body and who was so bandy-legged he could not ride a horse.

Clearly such a creature had no right to be King of England. It therefore followed that all monarchs since then were imposters – and so the crown should revert back to the last of the Tudors, Mr Anthony Hall.

From his campaign headquarters at the corner of Daws Road and St Owen Street, Hereford, he issued an open letter to King

Anthony Hall. (John Bull)

George, asking him to abdicate. He also held a series of public meetings throughout the Midlands, that in the Bull Ring, Birmingham, attracting a crowd of nearly 1,000 people. Many thought he looked the part, being handsome and over 6ft in height. He was always impeccably dressed and had the presence of a great actor. This was at the height of the Depression, and his promise of jobs and affordable houses for his people struck a chord with his audience. But there was a darker message too: an anti-German one. Many in the crowd had bitter memories of the war and he reminded them that the so-called royal family were German, though they had tried to hide that fact by changing their name from Saxe-Coburg-Gotha to Windsor.

His talks varied wildly in style: one minute he would ask, in a quite reasonable voice, whether the issue could be decided in the courts; the next he would declare that he would shoot the King as he would a dog. He also vowed to cut off the King's head. On another occasion he challenged King George to a duel, the loser to be beheaded. Finally, he dramatically claimed to be the first policeman to catch a criminal through the use of fingerprints. His local meetings, often held in St Peter's Square on a Saturday evening, became a popular rendezvous. He printed a genealogical chart, available for a penny, which demonstrated his claim.

When he started to issue his own banknotes, however, George V became concerned. It was only twelve years since the Russian royal family had been executed, after all. He asked that Hall be arrested and examined by two doctors – once Hall was officially declared insane, he could be confined to an institution. However, the doctors refused to make such

Hall banknote. (John Bull)

a declaration: one even said that Hall had a case of sorts. Now the King was really worried. He demanded that the full force of the law be brought against Anthony Hall, 'as long as it is quite understood that His Majesty is in no way responsible for the initiation of this.'

In the event, Hall was found guilty of using 'scandalous language', fined £10 and bound over to keep the peace. If he refused, he faced a fine of £25 or two months' imprisonment with hard labour. Mr Hall was also suffering from personal problems: his wife was asking for a divorce on the grounds of desertion. The stress became too much, and he at last retired to Little Dewchurch and the life of an ordinary citizen. In the Second World War he served his country as a shell examiner at the Rotherwas Munitions Factory.

He died in 1947 without male issue, and is buried in the small country churchyard of Little Dewchurch – rather than in St George's, Windsor, the last resting place of monarchs and the grave to which he thought himself entitled.

AD 1941

THE SPECIAL AIR SERVICE

IN EVERY PUB in Hereford there is, by some arcane military law, a morose man sitting in the corner who will, for the price of a pint, tell you about his experiences in the SAS. Real SAS men can be distinguished by their manly reticence and over-reliance on the SAS unofficial mottoes, 'If you haven't got a sense of humour you shouldn't have joined', and Long John Silver's motto, 'Them what dies will be the lucky ones.'

The unit was formed in North Africa in 1941 by David Stirling, who was fed-up with the foul-ups of larger operations and devised the fast-moving four-man patrol that is still a feature of the SAS today, made up of signaller, demolition expert, medic and linguist. The name was originally a piece of disinformation designed to make the Germans think it was purely a paratroop unit. Disbanded after the war, it was re-formed in 1947 when it was realised

that unpleasant local difficulties had not gone away. The beret was originally white but, after numerous fights between SAS soldiers and some Aussie troops taking the 'micky', it was replaced by the current beige colour.

Since 1960, 22 SAS, the regular army unit, has been based in Hereford. Originally at Bradbury Lines just south of the city, re-named Stirling Lines in 1984, this base had the disadvantage of having a footpath running through it and a railway line along one perimeter. In 2000 the regiment moved to a former RAF base at Credenhill.

It has four operational squadrons, each comprising approximately sixty men. The selection process, notoriously hard, takes place over four weeks and visits some of the more rugged parts of the Brecon Beacons and Black Mountains, usually with a 25kg pack on the back. The pass rate is only 5 per cent. Successful recruits can then wear the famous beret with winged dagger badge, giving the lie to the adage real men don't wear beige.

It would be possible to say much more about the SAS but such things are, of course, secret.

Panorama of the Brecon Beacons – now complete with dinosaur park – where the SAS train.

AD 1942

THE ROTHERWAS RAID

AT 6.30 A.M. on 27 July, a lone plane circled the munitions factory at Rotherwas. Many of those just getting off the buses in Holme Lacy Road, ready to start the morning shift, assumed that it was British and started to wave – but others recognised the sound of twin unsynchronised engines, and shouted, 'Get down, it's a Jerry!'

The bomber made its final approach from the south east. It dropped a stick of bombs and then headed south west. The first bomb landed on the Holme Lacy Road, near the bus stop, and killed seventeen people, with a further twenty-four injured. A friend of my mother had been to the hairdresser's the previous day. They found her in the rubble, face down, her hair-do intact and looking as if there was not a mark on her. However, when the rescuers turned her over the whole of her face was missing.

A second bomb hit a shed for storing bombs. Fortunately it was empty and, apart from the shed, no damage was done. But a third, heading for the transit shed, hit an iron girder and was deflected. Somehow it travelled 400 yards, hitting a house called Mansion Villas, just outside the western boundary of the factory. This was usually the home of Superintendent Hursey, in charge of the factory police, his wife and fifteen-year-old son Ken.

Tragically it was also home that night to the Hersey's elder son, home on leave from the RAF. His wife and mother-in-law were also staying. The bomb exploded, killing all the occupants except young Ken, who was pulled uninjured from the rubble.

A fourth bomb fell near a toilet block where Peggy Jones was washing off her protective make-up prior to going home. Knowing it was a German bomber overhead, she stood on a toilet seat to see what was happening. The next thing she remembered was sitting on the floor staring at the nose of a bomb. The resident bomb-disposal squad, known locally as the suicide squad, were quickly on the scene. To Peggy's doubtless relief, they realised that there was no danger from the explosive: the detonator was missing.

At the time of the raid the heavy machine-gun post in the centre of the factory was un-manned, it being thought that a raid was unlikely. Afterwards the story was put about that the bomber had been pursued by two Spitfires from Madley Aerodrome and shot down over the Bristol Channel, although this seems unlikely. Madley was mostly a training base, with few operational Spitfires. It was also suggested that this was not an intentional raid, but merely a lost bomber who saw something worth dropping his bombs on.

Rotherwas Munitions Factory. (Bustin Collection, Hereford Record Office)

Bomb damage at Rotherwas. (Bustin Collection, Hereford Record Office)

Certainly why only one bomber was used is a mystery if the Germans intended to inflict a great deal of damage.

Rotherwas Munitions Factory had been built on a green field site in 1916, to cope with the desperate need for artillery shells on the Western Front. While principally used for filling explosive shells, by the end of the war it was also filling mustard-gas shells. Controversially this seems to have continued in the inter-war years, despite Britain being a signatory to the Geneva Protocol that outlawed such weapons. As war became more likely in 1939, the factory was again put on a war footing and facilities for shell-filling increased, a process that was still mainly done by hand.

Enemy action was only one danger experienced at the factory. During the war there were five explosions at the factory, the first four killing eight people. But in May 1944 there was the biggest explosion in a munitions factory in Britain in the Second World War, probably caused by the desperate need for shells at that stage. A shell was seen to be smoking. The area was cleared whilst workers tried to deal with it: they delayed the explosion long enough for the building to be evacuated but one of their number, a Mr Morris, was killed. Desperate efforts were made to limit the fire but a second massive explosion killed a stretcher bearer. In all, the force of thirty-one 2,000lb bombs exploded. Shop windows as far away as the city centre were blown in and buildings damaged at Aylestone Hill. Five George Medals, an OBE, an MBE and nine BEMs were awarded to staff for their bravery.

Much of the damage was never repaired. After the war the site became an industrial estate and has recently been awarded Enterprise Zone status, with particular emphasis on the 'defence' industry.

BIBLIOGRAPHY

Andere, Mary, *Arthurian Links with Herefordshire* (Logaston Press, 1995)

Bannister, A., *Herefordshire and its Place in English History* (Jakeman & Carver, 1912)

Copplestone-Crow, Bruce, *Herefordshire Place Names* (Logaston Press, 2009)

Edmonds, John, *The History of Rotherwas Munitions Factory* (Logaston Press, 2004)

Fletcher, H.L.V., *Herefordshire* (Robert Hale, 1948)

Haggard, Andrew, *Dialect and Local Usages in Herefordshire* (Grower Books, 1972)

Heins, Nigel, *Flashback II* (Newsquest, no date)

Hill, Lt-Col, Tom, *Manu Forti* (Sutton, 1996)

Hodges, Geoffrey, *Ludford Bridge and Mortimer's Cross* (Logaston Press, 1989)

Hutchinson, John, *Herefordshire Biographies* (Jakeman & Carver, 1890)

Johnson, Andrew *et al*, *Aspects of Herefordshire* (Logaston Press, 1987)

Leather, Ella Mary, *Folklore of Herefordshire* (Jakeman & Carver, 1912)

Marshall, George, *The Cathedral Church of Hereford* (Littlebury & Co., no date)

Oppenheimer, Stephen, *Origins of the British* (Robinson Publishing, 2007)

Perry, Raymond, *Anglo-Saxon Herefordshire* (Oxengard Press, 2002)

Pevsner, Nikolaus, *Buildings of England: Herefordshire* (Penguin, 1963)

Phillott, Revd H.W., *Diocesan Histories: Hereford* (SPCK, 1888)

Rollason, David, *St Aethelbert of Hereford and the Cult of European Saints* (www.herefordcathedral.org)

Shakesheff, Timothy, *Rural Conflict, Crime and Punishment* (Boydell Press, 2003)

Shoesmith, Ron, *The Civil War in Hereford* (Logaston Press, 1995)

Sly, Nicola, *Herefordshire Murders* (The History Press, 2010)

Thurlby, Malcolm, *The Herefordshire School of Romanesque Sculpture* (Logaston Press, 1999)

Ward, Tim, *Roses Round the Door?* (Logaston Press, 2009)

West, John & Margaret, *A History of Herefordshire* (Phillimore, 1985)

Whitehead, David, *The Castle Green at Hereford* (Logaston Press, 2007)

If you enjoyed this book, you may also be interested in...

Herefordshire Folk Tales
DAVID PHELPS

This enchanting selection of thirty folk tales, the origins of which lie in the oral tradition, are full of Herefordian wit and wisdom, and are perfect for reading aloud or alone. Formed from early attempts to explain the natural and spiritual world, the tales range from the Saxon king of East Anglia who became the patron saint of Hereford Cathedral, to the story of the black hound of Baskerville Hall which inspired Arthur Conan Doyle. These stories have stood the test of time, and remain classic texts which will be enjoyed time and again by modern readers.

978 0 7524 4969 2

Haunted Hereford
DAVID PHELPS

For the unwary visitor, Hereford appears to be a peaceful place. But, for half its existence, it was a strategic centre in an often troubled and bloody border between England and Wales. It can be no surprise, then, that the city and surrounding countryside hide dark secrets. From the ghost of a verger who brought down the cathedral tower to the unquiet spirit of a careless chemist, the city has a rich history of spectral phenomena. Whether you are a tourist or resident, this book will make you look at the city with fresh eyes.

978 0 7524 6209 7

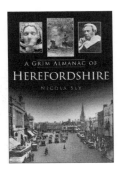

A Grim Almanac of Herefordshire
NICOLA SLY

A Grim Almanac of Herefordshire is a day-by-day catalogue of 365 ghastly tales from around the county, including stories of tragedy, torment and the truly unfortunate along with tales of murderers, bodysnatchers, duelists, poachers, rioters and rebels. There are accounts of tragic suicides, accidents and bizarre deaths, including the farmer bitten to death by his horse in 1887; and the young man from Colwall who allegedly sat on a spike. All these, plus tales of fires, catastrophes, explosions and disasters! Generously illustrated, this chronicle is an entertaining record of Herefordshire's grim past.

978 0 7524 5999 8

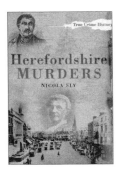

Herefordshire Murders
NICOLA SLY

This book will appeal to anyone interested in the shady side of Herefordshire's history. The county was home to infamous cases and also many lesser known murders, including the case of two-year-old Walter Frederick Steers, brutally killed in Little Hereford in 1891; eighty-seven-year-old Phillip Ballard, who died at the hands of two would-be burglars in Tupsley in 1887; and the shooting of two sisters at Burghill Court, near Hereford, by their butler in 1926.

978 0 7524 5360 6

Visit our website and discover thousands of other History Press books.

www.thehistorypress.co.uk